GREAT SMOKY
MOUNTAINS
TRIVIA

DORIS GOVE

RIVERBEND
PUBLISHING

ACKNOWLEDGMENTS

Thanks to Ken McFarland for checking the plant chapter and to B. J. Brooks for checking the geology facts. The following people helped with ideas and suggestions: John Finger, Norwood Gove, Ruth Gove, Nancy Gray of the National Park Service, Lee Knight, Jim Lowe, Jeff Mellor, Susan Rudolph, Cindy Spangler, and Merikay Waldvogel. Special thanks to Janet Spencer for encouragement and feedback. Thanks also to naturalists, writers, researchers, and fellow hikers who have taught me to see the mountains.

Great Smoky Mountains Trivia
Copyright © 2010 by Doris Gove
Published by Riverbend Publishing, Helena, Montana

ISBN 13: 978-1-60639-017-7

Printed in the United States of America.

4 5 6 7 8 9 SB 26 25 24 23 22 21

Cover design by Bob Smith
Text design by Barbara Fifer

Riverbend Publishing
P.O. Box 5833
Helena, MT 59604
1-866-787-2363
www.riverbendpublishing.com

CONTENTS

GREAT SMOKY MOUNTAINS NATIONAL PARK HISTORY

Q. Which American president authorized the formation of a national park in the Great Smoky Mountains?
A. Calvin Coolidge, in 1926.

Q. How long did it take for the park to be actually established?
A. Eight years, until 1934.

Q. What took so long?
A. The land was privately owned, in parcels ranging from tiny vacation lots to large apple orchards, to communities, to huge timber holdings. None of the owners were eager to have a park on their land.

Big Dates for the Park

1923 Mrs. Ann Davis, after a trip to western national parks, wonders, why not have a park in the Great Smokies? Later, as one of Tennessee's first female state representatives, she introduces a bill to establish a park.

1926 Congress passes a bill to create two parks in the South, Smokies and Shenandoah, but stipulates that the states provide the land. President Calvin Coolidge signs it.

1927 John D. Rockefeller, Jr., promises $5 million to match the states' funds for land purchases.

1931 Tennessee and North Carolina present deeds to the federal government.

1933 The Civilian Conservation Corps starts working on roads, trails, campgrounds, and visitor facilities.

June 15, 1934 Congress establishes Great Smoky Mountains National Park.

September 2, 1940 President Franklin D. Roosevelt dedicates the park at the Rockefeller Memorial at Newfound Gap, with over 10,000 spectators.

1941 Annual visitation to the Smokies tops one million.

1942-1945 The Tennessee Valley Authority buys land in North Carolina to build Fontana Dam, the highest dam in the East, to generate power for the war effort in Oak Ridge and other sites. They transfer 44,000 acres (17,800 hectares) along the north shore of Fontana Lake to the national park.

"I hope...that one hundred years from now the Great Smoky National Park will still belong in practice, as well as in theory, to the people of a free nation."—Franklin Roosevelt, 1940

Q. So who did want a park?

A. Business people who saw a park as a way to attract tourism, conservationists who saw the beauty of the mountains, and automobile associations who wanted to encourage auto touring.

Q. When did the Smoky Mountains become "Great?"

A. Some early writers called the Smokies "Great," but it became official when the park advocates hired a New York PR firm to help them in the 1920s.

Seven unusual facts about the establishment of GSMNP:

1. It was the first park in which the land was purchased from many private owners and communities.

2. It was the first park that used eminent domain (forced sale) for that purpose.

3. It was the first park in which ordinary citizens worked and contributed money towards its establishment.

4. It's the only U.S. national park shared almost evenly by two states.

5. It's the second U.S. national park established east of the Mississippi (the first was Acadia National Park, in Maine, 1919).

6. It's the only park that allowed logging to continue after the official park designation, because the Little River Lumber Company sold its land at an affordable Depression-era price only under the condition that they could keep logging for five years.

7. It's the only park in which two states deeded land to the federal government for the purpose of establishing a park.

Q. Park supporters almost failed to raise enough money to buy the land needed for the park, partly because of the hardships of the Great Depression and partly because so many landowners sued to prevent eminent domain. What saved the project?

A. A government bailout of $1.5 million and an additional gift from John D. Rockefeller to reach the amount to match his original $5 million pledge.

GSMNP history was featured in the 2009 PBS documentary The National Parks: America's Best Idea *by Ken Burns.*

Albright (left) with President Herbert Hoover, an avid trout fisher.

Q. Who was Horace Albright?
A. The second director of the National Park Service and a friend of John D. Rockefeller, Jr. Albright Grove, one of the most beautiful areas of old-growth forest in the park, is named for him.

Q. Which state has a larger portion of land?
A) Tennessee
B) North Carolina
C) The two states match, acre for acre
A. B) North Carolina has about 3% more land in the park than Tennessee.

Q. How was Roosevelt's dedication talk broadcast?
A. Civilian Conservation Corps (CCC) boys draped 14 miles of wire through the woods from Gatlinburg to Newfound Gap and guarded the wires during the ceremony. NBC and CBS aired the speeches.

Q. How did Roosevelt get to Newfound Gap?
A. From the Knoxville train station he rode in an open 12-cylinder Packard with Secret Service agents on the running boards.

Q. Where did Roosevelt stand during his dedication speech?
A. With one foot in North Carolina and the other in Tennessee.

> Roosevelt couldn't walk well because of polio; for many park spectators, this was the first time they observed that he had to be helped to the lectern, though a special ramp was built to conceal that fact. Photographers respected the President's wishes and took no pictures of people helping him.

Q. What was the main topic of Roosevelt's speech?

FDR dedicated GSMNP "For the permanent enjoyment of all the people."

A. He first mentioned other national parks that would soon join the Smokies, then talked about threats to American freedom.

> #### From FDR's dedication speech
>
> "We used up or destroyed much of our natural heritage just because that heritage was so bountiful. We slashed our forests, we used our soils, we encouraged floods, we overconcentrated our wealth, we disregarded our unemployed—all of this so greatly that we were brought rather suddenly to face the fact that unless we gave thought to the lives of our children and grandchildren, they would no longer be able to live and to improve upon our American way of life.
>
> "I hope...that one hundred years from now the Great Smoky National Park will still belong in practice, as well as in theory, to the people of a free nation....
>
> "The winds that blow through the wide sky in these mountains, the winds that sweep from Canada to Mexico, from the Pacific to the Atlantic—have always blown on free men. We are free today. If we join together now—men and women and children—to face the common menace as a united people, we shall be free tomorrow. So, to the free people of America, I dedicate this Park."

Q. Did John D. Rockefeller Jr. help establish any other national parks?

A. Yes, many, including Grand Teton, Acadia, Yosemite, Shenandoah. His philanthropy had a strong conservation focus.

Q. Which of the following other causes did Rockefeller influence?

    A) Repeal of prohibition   B) Development of birth control
    C) The United Nations

A. All three. He advocated repeal of prohibition, though he never drank alcohol, because of the crime that prohibition fostered. He supported the work of Margaret Sanger, a birth-control pioneer, and he donated land in Manhattan where the United Nations now stands.

In 1972, Congress authorized the John D. Rockefeller, Jr., Memorial Highway to honor his conservation philanthropy. This scenic road connects Yellowstone National Park to Grand Teton National Park.

Q. Rockefeller gave $5 million; how much did Tennessee school children contribute to the establishment of the park?
A. $1,391.72 was contributed by 4,500 children, mostly nickels, dimes, and pennies. Kids that gave a dollar got a Park Founder certificate.

Q. Who else contributed?
A. Church groups, community groups, automobile associations, hiking and civic clubs, the governments of Tennessee and North Carolina, of Knoxville and Asheville, and individuals.

Q. What is the entrance fee for the Smokies?
A. The park's charter states that no entrance fee will ever be charged because of citizens' role in park creation.

Q. If there's no entrance fee, how can the park get extra funds?
A. Two organizations raise funds for the Smokies. The Great Smoky Mountains Association (SmokiesInformation.org), established in 1950, raises funds by publishing and selling books and other publications. GSMA runs the visitor centers, and the profit from sales goes back into the park to support trail work, hiring of seasonal employees (for example, the millers in the Cable Mill in Cades Cove and Mingus Mill), building projects such as the new Oconaluftee Visitor Center.

Friends of the Smokies (FOTS, www.friends ofthesmokies.org) started in 1996 with a project to restore the Mount Cammerer Fire tower and since then have raised millions to support the park.

In 2009, Dolly Parton released a CD, *Sha-Kon-O-Hey: Land of Blue Smoke,* and produced a show about settlers leaving their land to make a park. Profits from the CD go to Trails Forever, an FOTS endowment program to maintain and improve Smokies trails.

Q. How many people had to leave their homes and livelihoods to make way for the park?

"The Smoky Mountains have inspired me and my music since I was a little girl. They touch my soul and lift my spirits."—
Dolly Parton, Ambassador for the park's 75th anniversary

A. More than 5,000, mostly farmers and families that worked in low- or mid-elevation communities such as Cades Cove, Sugarlands, Greenbrier, Cataloochee.

One family was forced to leave Greenbrier by the Park Service. They moved to Norris, Tennessee. When the Tennessee Valley Authority removed people to build their first dam in Norris, the same family moved to the sleepy town of Oak Ridge, just in time to be displaced by the Manhattan Project. They finally moved to Pigeon Forge.

Q. Which was the largest community?
A. Cataloochee Valley, with 1,200 people, three schools, churches, stores, and acres of apple orchards.

Q. Did most of the residents resist leaving?
A. No. About two-thirds left voluntarily. Life was hard in the mountains, and many families had so many children that their land could no longer support new generations of families. In many cases, the mountain soils had become depleted. But for prosperous communities like Cataloochee and Cades Cove, leaving was painful.

The last residents of the park were Kermit and Lois Caughron. They stayed in Cades Cove with a lifetime lease, kept beef cattle, sold honey to tourists, had a gasoline-powered washing machine and a kerosene refrigerator. Kermit died in 1999.

The last Cataloochee resident, Uncle Steve Woody, left in 1942.

Copper mining
A prospector found a rich vein of copper ore on the Sugar Fork of Hazel Creek. W. S. Adams, a New York investor, bought the land and sank shafts and opened a mining village. Before he could get any ore out or build a smelter, George Westfeldt of New Orleans sued, saying he had claimed the land right after the Civil War. The suit lasted 26 years, one of the longest in American legal history, and when it was finally decided in favor of Adams, both men were dead. Adams' heirs started sinking shafts in 1942, just in time for

"We must preserve...an appreciation of the sacrifices of these people, who, even under protest, gave up their lands..."—Randolph Shields, Maryville College instructor born in Cades Cove, 1913

TVA to condemn the land because of the wartime urgency to build Fontana Dam.

Old mining shafts in the Hazel Creek area of the park are closed to the public.

Q. What did the park look like in 1934?
A. Many parts of it were a mess. Logging companies had left scarred hillsides, huge erosion gullies, and polluted streams. Fires had spread from logged areas to the tops of Charlies Bunion and Brushy Mountain. Only about a third of the new park had good forest left. It was a fixer-upper.

Q. Who did the fixing?
A. Civilian Conservation Corps (jokingly, "Roosevelt's Tree Army") planted trees; built roads, visitor centers, trails and bridges; stopped erosion; and built the Rockefeller Monument at Newfound Gap.

CCC workers in the Smokies.

Q. When did Roosevelt propose the establishment of the Civilian Conservation Corps, or CCC?
A. In the first week of his presidency in 1931.

Q. Who were the CCC workers?
A. Young men who had tried and failed to get work, had families, and were willing to sign on for at least six months. CCC workers got room, board, education, and health care.

Q. How much did they earn?
A. $30/month, of which they could keep $5. The rest was sent home to their families. During the Great Depression, this Public Works Administration program supported families, provided training and education for participants, and got a lot of work done that we still see today.

Q. Who was the oldest CCC boy in Great Smoky Mountains National Park?

CCC camps in the Smokies had libraries, competitive sports teams, classes from basic literacy to auto mechanics, newspapers, and holiday parties, along with the hard work.

A. Aden Carver, who was born in Smokemont in 1844. At age 90 he joined a CCC crew and helped restore the Mingus Mill, which he had helped build it in 1856. He died in 1945 at age 101.

> A farmer in South Carolina worked hard to earn enough money during the Depression to send his sons to college. Halfway through the youngest son's freshman year, the farmer received the grades—they were bad. He took the train down to the college town, found the son at a party, took him by the ear back to the station, took another train to a CCC camp in the Smokies, and enrolled the boy. After two years of rock work, the young man reenrolled in college and did quite well.

Q. How many U.S. presidents have visited the Smokies while in office?
A. Only one, at the time of this writing: Franklin D. Roosevelt. George W. Bush attempted to visit Cades Cove for Earth Day in 2005. Thunderstorms prevented his helicopter from leaving the Knoxville airport. Eleanor Roosevelt visited the Smokies a few times, once staying at the Ekaneetlee Lodge in Cades Cove.

Q. Which of the following was proposed during the early years of managing the Great Smoky Mountains National Park?
A) A lake in Cades Cove, made by damming Abrams Creek.
B) A skyline drive like the one in Shenandoah National Park.
C) Killing of water snakes so there would be more trout.
A. All three.

Q. What happened to those plans?
A. The Great Depression, then the end of CCC programs, and World War II slowed down those grand plans and others, including big hotels and amphitheaters. And rangers learned to appreciate the snakes.

Q. How many superintendents has the park had?
A. 15.

More than 4,000 CCC enrollees worked in the Smokies.

Q. How many of them were women?
A. One so far—Karen Wade, from 1994 to 1999. She moved from the largest American national park (Wrangell–St. Elias in Alaska) to the most-visited one.

Q. Who was the first Smokies superintendent?
A. J. Ross Eakin, from 1931-1945. He started with two rangers, one for Tennessee and one for North Carolina, and some big problems: poachers, moonshiners, squatters, and residents who wouldn't leave.

Q. Where is the park superintendent's office?
A. In the Park Headquarters building behind the Sugarlands Visitor Center. It was built by the CCC from stone quarried near Ravensford, on the North Carolina side of the park, and the lobby is paneled with wormy chestnut from trees that were cut after the chestnut blight killed them.

Q. Where do biologists and other researchers have their offices?
A. In a modern facility of labs, offices, and greenhouses on Twin Creeks Trail, near the Bud Ogle Homesite and Nature Trail.

Q. On June 13, 2009, as part of the 75th Anniversary celebration, the Knoxville Symphony Orchestra performed in Cades Cove. Who was their guest concert pianist?
A. U.S. Senator Lamar Alexander, (R) Tennessee

Q. How many people attended the open air concert?
A. 6,500

Q. Who was the guest pianist for the 50th Anniversary concert in 1984?
A. Tennessee Governor Lamar Alexander

Q. Who was the ambassador for the park during its 75th Anniversary year in 2009?
A. Dr. Dolly Parton

The CCC program ended in July, 1942.

Q. Dr. Dolly?

A. Dolly Parton received an Honorary Doctorate in Humane and Musical Letters from the University of Tennessee on May 8, 2009 in recognition of her role as cultural ambassador, philanthropist, and lifelong advocate for education. She founded the Imagination Library, which sends a book every month from birth to age five to each child, at their homes, in communities that enroll and purchase the books. By 2009, 20 million books had been sent to children in Tennessee, 47 other states, the  United Kingdom, and Canada. The Foundation supports local schools and provides incentives for graduation and college scholarships. Dr. Dolly has also received a Woodrow Wilson Award for Public Service, a National Medal of Arts, seven Grammys, two Oscar nominations, and the 2009 International Heartbeat Award.

She is the only the fourth recipient of an honorary doctorate from the University of Tennessee—the third recipient was U.S. Senator Howard Baker Jr. in 2005.

Q. Who rededicated the park on September 2, 2009, at the Rockefeller Monument?

A. Ken Salazar, Secretary of Interior, the governors of Tennessee and North Carolina, the U.S. Senators of Tennessee and North Carolina, the U.S. Representatives from the counties surrounding the park, Cherokee tribal leaders, Great Smokies park superintendent Dale Ditmanson, Dr. Dolly Parton, local dignitaries, a few people who attended the original event in 1940, a few folks who had to leave their land to make way for the park, a few CCC men who worked on trails and roads and bridges in the 1930s, two marching bands, and 2,000 invited guests.

Q. How many people volunteered in the park in 2008?

A. 2,777; volunteer hours equaled 117,500. Volunteer services to the park are the fourth largest in the National Park Service.

"We feel like we own [the park] because our families did...And we are proud we gave this park to the country for others to enjoy."
—U.S. Senator Lamar Alexander, Sept. 2, 2009

Some examples of volunteer activities:
• Trail maintenance
• Visitor Center desk information
• Giving out backcountry permits and advice
• Campground host
• Citizen Science—help with plant or animal research (including Beetle Blitzes, Fern Forays, and Slime Mold Surveys)
• Interpretive programs
• Teaching lessons in period costume at Little Greenbrier Schoolhouse
• Mapping trails and cemeteries with GPS equipment
• Monitoring the elk in Cataloochee Elk Bugle Corps

Q. What is the Student Conservation Association?
A. The Student Conservation Association provides organized Spring and Fall Break projects in trail maintenance or exotic plant control for college students, and also summer internships. Many of the students go on to jobs in national parks.

You should thank one volunteer for accurate trail mileages on Smokies maps and trail signs. In 1994, **Bob Lochbaum,** a retired Oak Ridge engineer, started measuring trails. First, of course, he studied the problem and determined the most precise way to measure with a calibrated wheel (What do you do with your wheel when you cross a creek? What's the best tire pressure for the wheel? How do you avoid errors caused by parallax when climbing?). He measured every trail in the park 10 times or so, in both directions, with a maximum error of 15 inches/mile, or 0.025%. He developed a complicated computer program to keep track of it all. The park gave him a sophisticated GPS with a battery backpack, so he could check everything again—including landmarks, cemeteries, and other sites. The GPS records a three-dimensional position every five seconds.

Retired schoolteacher **Robin Goddard** has volunteered in the park since 1969. On Tuesdays she portrays a 1900s schoolteacher at the Little Greenbrier School near Metcalf

---

The park has Adopt-a-trail, Adopt-a-campsite ,and Volunteers in the Park (VIP) volunteer programs.

Bottoms. If you decide to visit, brush up on your spelling first or you may have to stay after school. She gets 500 to 700 visitors on some summer Tuesdays, her regular days.

Robin Goddard's husband, Jim, spent 100 days a year for a few years working on the Appalachian Trail in remote sections—where you have to hike 15-20 miles before you can even start working.

Q. How long was the school year in the mountains?
A. Usually two or three months. Children had to help on the farm the rest of the time.

Q. Are there any hotels left in the Smokies?
A. No, the last hotel, Wonderland in Elkmont, closed in 1992. A wilderness lodge accommodates hikers and provide meals on Mount Le Conte.

Q. How do we get there?
A. Hike, either five miles up Alum Cave Trail or somewhat longer hikes from Cherokee Orchard or Newfound Gap. The lodge is popular, and reservations have to be made far in advance. It has room for 50 guests at a time and provides dinner and breakfast.

Q. How does the lodge get supplies?
A. Llamas bring clean laundry and other supplies Monday, Wednesday, and Friday up Trillium Gap Trail. Fuel and bulk supplies (including a couple of tons of pancake mix) arrive by helicopter when the season opens in the spring. Lodge workers run down and up Alum Cave Trail for "emergency" supplies, such as beer and pizza.

Q. Why llamas?
A. The lodge used to use horses, but they tore up the trail. Llama hooves spread when they step and do very little trail damage.

Q. What new service did Le Conte Lodge start in 2009?
A. A sit-down or packed lunch, reservations required, and hot chocolate and baked goods for sale.

_____

"In this Park, we shall conserve these trees, the pine, the red-bud, the dogwood, the azalea, the rhododendron, the trout and the thrush for the happiness of the American people."—FDR

Q. Who was Cumberland Jack?

A. A black German shepherd police dog that helped the first caretaker of Le Conte Lodge, Paul Adams. Adams would put money and a list in Jack's saddlebags and send him down to Ogle's store in Gatlinburg for mail and up to 30 pounds of supplies. When Adams and Jack went to town together, Jack would always carry the money because Adams got robbed once.

Le Conte Lodge is the highest lodge east of the Mississippi, at 6593 feet (2009.5 m). Le Conte is the tallest (not highest in elevation) mountain in the east since it is 5301 feet (1615.7 m) from its base in Gatlinburg. The lodge has no electricity but has delicious spring water.

The first operator of Le Conte Lodge, Jack Huff, carried his mother to the top of Le Conte. She sat in a small chair strapped to his back and faced backward all the way up. You can see photos of Jack and his mother in the lodge social room.

The Park Commission invited **Clarence Darrow** to visit Elkmont in 1925 because they felt it would get national publicity for the park movement. Darrow and his client, John Scopes. traveled from the Dayton Scopes Monkey Trial, along with several reporters from national newspapers, and Darrow spoke in favor of the park effort. William Jennings Bryan, the prosecuting attorney (who actually won the Scopes trial) was also invited, but he suffered a fatal heart attack in Dayton at the end of the trial.

Q. What is "the Purchase"?

A. The Purchase was a gift of 574 acres of land at Purchase Knob

---

Gatlinburg was named for Radford Gatlin, who opened a store and post office there before the Civil War. Gatlin, who owned a slave and joined the Confederacy, was not welcomed back after the war.

in 2000, adjacent to the park in North Carolina. The donors were Kathryn McNeil and Voit Gilmore. It is now home to the Appalachian Highlands Science Learning Center, with offices, laboratories, and lodging for students or researchers.

Q. How many people visit the Smokies each year?
A. More than 9 million—more than any other national park.

Q. How much do visitors add to the local economy?
A. An estimated $800 million per year—about twice the amount for Grand Canyon, the next most visited park.

Q. How many units are there of the National Park Service?
A. 392, as of October 28, 2009, when Port Chicago Naval Magazine National Memorial in California was added to the NPS.

Q. What was the first national park?
A. Yellowstone, in 1872. Yosemite was set aside as a wilderness park by President Abraham Lincoln in 1864 but administered by California until it became a national park in 1890.

Q. Which American president created the National Park Service?
A. Woodrow Wilson

Q. Which of the following is not managed by the National Park Service?
   A) Washington Monument   B) Niagara Falls   C) Mount Rainier
A. B) Niagara Falls. And, in fact, the commercialization of Niagara Falls prompted many people to try to preserve beautiful places and natural areas.

Q. Forty-nine states have national parks or units of the National Park Service. Which is the only state that does not?
A. Delaware.

The National Park Service Act of 1916 was expanded in 1970 to provide equal status and protection to national parks, monuments, historic sites, seashores, rivers, trails, cemeteries, and other units.

Q. What two units of the NPS connect GSMNP to Shenandoah National Park?
A. Appalachian Trail and Blue Ridge Parkway

Q. How long did it take to build the Blue Ridge Parkway?
A. 52 years, starting in 1935 with several CCC crews.
Q. How many fire towers did the CCC build to watch for fire in the Smokies?
A. Fifteen, arranged so that at least two overlapped each view, in order that fire or smoke could be located by triangulation. Two towers were outside the park.

Q. Most of the towers were metal frames with several flights of steps up to a cabin to give a view over the trees. Which fire tower is round and only one story taller than the rock it's built on?
A. Mount Cammerer, built in the 1930s and rebuilt by Friends of the Smokies in 1996. The CCC built it of rock quarried a little way down the mountain. By the way, Mount Cammerer provides one of the best fall color views in the Smokies.

Q. What equipment did fire watchers have?
A. Binoculars, radio, and an alidade (remember this word for your next Scrabble game), which is a combination compass and sighter. They also carried panoramic maps, topographical maps, and two week's worth of food.

Q. What were fire watchers instructed to do in violent thunderstorms?
A. Stay right up there in the tower and watch for lightning strikes.

Q. Was that safe?
A. Probably not. In one case, everything inside a tower cabin was burned in a lightning strike. For some reason, the fire watcher was not present at the time.

Q. How many fire towers remain in the Smokies?
A. Five. The towers were manned until 1953. Some were dis-

"When I went south into these mountains, I was seeking a Back of Beyond."—Horace Kephart, 1904

mantled for safety. The Cove Mountain Tower was converted to an air-quality monitoring station. Hikers can climb Shuckstack, Mount Sterling, and Mount Cammerer towers.

Q. When did Smokey Bear start telling people about fire danger?
A. 1944. He was a cartoon bear used in a campaign to protect national forests from human-caused fires.

Q. Did Smokey Bear get his name from the Smoky Mountains?
A. No. The live Smokey Bear was a cub who survived a 1950 forest fire in New Mexico, and was nicknamed "Hotfoot Teddy." After getting veterinary burn care, he was recovering with a rancher's family when newspapers publicized his story and he was renamed "Smokey Bear." The cub soon was moved to the National Zoo in Washington, D.C., where he stayed until dying in 1976.

Q. Where's Smokey Bear been—haven't heard much from him lately.
A. Park management has changed—foresters now recognize that fire has a beneficial place in nature. In the Smokies, fires may be set in some areas to prevent buildup of brush and more severe fires later. When fires are detected, park managers decide whether or not to fight them.

Cherokees and settlers may have kept the balds open with fire, and Cades Cove residents improved blueberry crops by burning dry hillsides in the fall.

Q. Who was Horace Kephart?
A. Horace Kephart was a successful writer, scholar, and librarian. He had studied at Harvard and in Italy, had translated Dante into English and learned Finnish, and he lived in St. Louis with his wife and six children. However, in 1904, struggling with alcoholism and conflicts at home, he left a prestigious job and came east seeking a "back of beyond." He arrived by train in Bushnell, North Carolina, too drunk to stand.

"I owe my life to these mountains and I want them preserved so that others may profit as I have."—Horace Kephart

Q. Then what happened?

A. Granville Calhoun, a resident of Medlin, N.C., picked Kephart up at the train station, draped him over a mule, took him home and nursed him back to health. Kephart then retreated into the mountains for three years, met many moonshiners, but managed to sober up. He wrote two best selling books: *Camping and Woodcraft* and *Our Southern Highlanders*, both of which are still in print today. He moved to Bryson City and wrote magazine articles about Smokies scenery, people, plants and animals, hunting and fishing. In the 1920s, Kephart started advocating for a national park.

> "Scholar, Author, Outdoorsman. He loved his neighbors and pictured them in Our Southern Highlanders. His vision helped create the Great Smoky Mountains National Park."—*Inscription on Kephart's grave on School House Hill, Bryson City, 1931*

Q. What happened to Kephart's abandoned family?

A. Laura Mack Kephart moved the four girls and two boys to Ithaca, New York, and put all six children through Cornell University.

> In 1919 Horace Kephart wrote three magazine articles for *Outing Magazine* titled "The Cherokees of the Smoky Mountains: A Little Band that has Stood Against the White Tide for Three Hundred Years." Laura Mack Kephart, impoverished after Kephart's death, published the articles as a booklet and made only a few dollars. You can buy the booklet now at Smokies visitor centers.

Q. Kephart worked with George Masa, a photographer, to garner public support for a park. Where did Masa come from?

A. George Masa left Japan to study mining in the U.S., but could not find work as a mining engineer. He worked as a valet at the Grove Park Inn in Asheville. As he learned English and photography, he became popular with the clients, taking them on tours and developing their pictures. In his spare time, he hiked and photographed the Smokies.

Because of divided loyalties, the Civil War hurt many families in the mountains, but the main effect of the war was hardship because of raiders.

Q. Kephart and Masa documented the beauty of the mountains and the destruction by logging companies. What were some of the most destructive and dangerous practices?

A. **Skidding**—huge trees were dragged by horses or overhead cables to the nearest rail line.

Ball-hooting—trees on a ridge top or high slope were pushed and rolled down, tearing up the hillside on the way.

Splash dams—a dam was built in a creek valley to make a temporary lake, which was then filled with logs. Then the dam was opened or dynamited to flush the logs downstream. Sometimes two or three dams would be dynamited at intervals to get the logs farther.

Slash—the loggers did not bother to remove branches or small trees from the logging site, and fires would start and spread in this debris.

Q. Kephart wrote books, magazine articles, and pamphlets on many historical and cultural topics. He wrote one book of fiction called *Smoky Mountain Magic* with a dramatic plot including a mystery, a beautiful botanist, a witch, Cherokee legends and Little People, valuable gems, and a cliffhanger in a cave. When was it published?

A. In 2009, nearly 80 years after Kephart's death. His granddaughter found the manuscript among his papers and showed it to Dale Ditmanson, Smokies Superintendent. The Great Smoky Mountains Association published the book, and it is selling well.

Union Colonel George Kirk raided Cataloochee in what may have been the last skirmishes of the war, after Lee surrendered.

Mountain Culture

Q. How long have people lived in the Smoky Mountains?
A. Probably more than 10,000 years.

Q. The Cherokee have been here that long?
A. No, the Cherokee are relative newcomers. They replaced the Woodland Indians about 1,000 years ago. They came down from the north. The Cherokee language is related to Iroquois.

Q. Who was the first European explorer to meet the Cherokee?
A. Hernando de Soto, exploring for Spain, in 1540.

Q. De Soto wanted gold from the Cherokees. What did he get?
A. A bison skin.

Q. What collegiate sport comes from Cherokee traditions?
A. Lacrosse. Cherokees called it "Little Brother of War," and the rules apparently were: get the ball to the goal by whatever means possible.

Q. Where was the largest Cherokee town in the Smokies area?
A. Just outside the current park boundary on Deep Creek in North Carolina. The town was called Kituwah, and there were many smaller towns along the Oconaluftee River. Cherokee hunters used the park, and they believed that there was a magic lake at Clingmans Dome. If a wounded bear or deer jumped into the lake, it would emerge healed.

The Cherokees did not spend much time high in the mountains, but if they did, they might run into the Little People, the *Nunnehi* of Cherokee legend. The Little People lived in a reverse world (very much like ours, but the seasons were reversed—you could tell, because springs ran between the two worlds, and they were always cold in summer and warm in winter). Nunnehi maidens would sometimes lure Cherokee hunters a long way from home and then make themselves invisible as they slipped back through a spring to the other world.

Q. What did the Cherokees build their teepees out of?
A. Cherokees never lived in teepees. They built wood-frame houses covered with vines and mud or clay. Family houses surrounded a large council house to make up a village. Later, when Cherokees got saws and other tools from white settlers, they built log houses.

In 1776, white soldiers burned all the Cherokee towns and crops they could find along the rivers coming out of the mountains as a punishment for the Cherokees siding with the English.

Q. A mountain in the Smokies, the biggest tree in the world, a nuclear power plant, and many schools are named for a Cherokee man named George Gist, or Sequoyah. What did he do?
A. Sequoyah (spellings vary, but it's the same man) developed an alphabet (or syllabary, if you want to be precise) of 86 characters for the Cherokee language in 1830. It is the only time known in human history when one person accomplished such a thing. At the time, Sequoyah and his tribespeople were illiterate. Within two years, the Cherokees published a newspaper in their own language (*The Phoenix*) and most Cherokees could read it.

Sequoyah (1776-1843) spent 12 years developing his writing system for the Cherokee language.

Q. Where can we see Sequoyah's alphabet?

A. Any street sign in the town of Cherokee. Or ask any Cherokee first grader. Or hike Oconaluftee Trail from the visitor center to Cherokee.

Q. Sequoyah called his syllabary "Talking Leaves," and his people (including his wife) were suspicious and accused him of sorcery. How did he convince them of the power of the talking leaves?

A. He sent his 12-year-old daughter, who had learned the syllabary, across the village with some women. He then wrote a message to her that was carried by one of the accusers. The

message? "I'm thirsty!" The girl ran and got him a cup of water.

Many Native Americans have lost much of their culture, language, and traditions. However, when Cherokee Medicine Men learned Sequoyah's written Cherokee language, some of them recorded myths, medicinal knowledge, and Sacred Formulas in notebooks. These records were closely guarded secrets, but a young ethnologist named James Mooney gained the trust of a Cherokee man named Swimmer, who had recorded Cherokee beliefs on diseases and cures, prescriptions, color symbolism, sacred numbers, little people, and burial practices. Swimmer's manuscripts have been published and are used by modern Cherokees.

Q. Who was Return Jonathan Meigs?

A. A government surveyor who surveyed a line between Indian lands and lands open to European settlement in 1802. The boundary was pretty much ignored and was later dissolved by treaties. Meigs surveyed from Mount Collins (near Clingmans Dome) to a small mountain where he stationed someone to wave a blanket,

---

An outdoor drama in Cherokee, Unto These Hills, *tells stories from Cherokee culture, and has played during the summer since 1950.*

thus naming Blanket Mountain, near Elkmont. (And why was his first name Return? Apparently, Return's father had to pop the question several times; each time the lady said no but encouraged him to return.)

Q. What happened to the Cherokee as white settlers were moving into the south?
A. In the Revolutionary War, the Cherokee sided with the British. American soldiers destroyed Cherokee villages and took more land from the tribe. Later, through more treaties, Cherokees lost even more land. In the 1830s, under the Indian Removal Act, President Andrew Jackson (who had fought beside Cherokee allies in the Creek War of 1813-1814) oversaw the removal of Indians of the southeast U.S. to Oklahoma. Beginning in 1831 with the Choctaws (and subsequently the Seminoles, Creeks, and Chickasaws), the march west became known as the "Trail of Tears." In 1838, General Winfield Scott and his troops rounded up most of the Cherokees, locked them in stockades and in the fall marched them out. An estimated 25% of all tribes died in the march west.

Q. How did the Cherokee in North Carolina avoid the Trail of Tears?
A. There are many versions to the story. T'Sali and his family, one of the last groups to be rounded up, started off peacefully as soldiers prodded them and burnt their houses as soon as they were vacated. But along the way, a soldier poked T'Sali's wife with a bayonet. T'Sali and the other men revolted, turned on the soldiers, killed one, and escaped into the Smokies. General Scott said that if T'Sali and his sons would surrender, he would not pursue the others. T'Sali and his sons walked out, stood beside waiting graves, and were shot, except for the littlest boy. Soldiers forced other Cherokees to carry out the execution. The families remaining in the Smoky Mountains became the core of the Eastern Band of the Cherokee Nation.

Q. How did they get their land in Cherokee back?
A. Another good story. Chief Yonaguska adopted a white boy, Will Thomas. Thomas became a lawyer and, before Yonaguska died, he appointed Thomas hereditary chief, the only white man ever given

---

In 1939, 100 years after T'Sali was shot, high school students built a monument to him in Gatlinburg. Look for it in a small park by the river.

that honor. As a white man, Thomas could hold deeds, and the Cherokee transferred their lands to him. In the 1920s, the law was changed, and Thomas restored the land to Cherokee ownership.

Q. So Cherokees became full citizens then?
A. In theory, yes; in practice, Cherokees were not allowed to vote until after World War II, when they came back as veterans.

A good book based on the life of **Will Thomas** and his life between the white and Cherokee cultures and his efforts to save the Cherokee: *Thirteen Moons*, by Charles Frazier (2006). (Frazier also wrote the popular novel *Cold Mountain*. The actual Cold Mountain is not in the Smokies, but you can see it from Hemphill Bald or Mount Sterling.) Frazier draws heavily from the writings of William Bartram, a botanist who described the marvelous biodiversity of the southern Appalachians.

Q. Who were the first white settlers of Gatlinburg, then called White Oak Flats?
A. A widow, Martha Jane Huskey Ogle and her seven children.

Rainbow by Moonlight by Loletta Clouse (2009) is a romantic novel about a young woman who came to Gatlinburg in the 1920s to teach at the settlement school. One of the characters in the book was a real employee at the school: Aunt Lizzie Reagan, who was hired to cook and clean, but ended up reviving weaving skills that were being abandoned by the mountain women.

Q. Who was Hairy John Walker?
A. A settler in the Metcalf Bottoms who, after serving as a Union soldier and being a captive in the Confederates' Andersonville

---

Thomas Divide, a long ridge from the Smokies Crest to Cherokee, is named for Will Thomas.

Prison, married Margaret Jane King in 1866, whom he had started courting before the Civil War. They had four sons and seven daughters. Hairy John Walker died in 1921.

Q. What knocked several rocks off the Walker family chimney in 1925?

A) An earthquake.   B) A marauding bear

C) A rejected suitor   D) An outbuilding lifted by a tornado

A. A) An earthquake.

Q. Who were the Walker Sisters?

A. After the park was created in 1934, five of Hairy John and Margaret Jane Walker's daughters stayed in the park in a cabin in Little Greenbrier, near Metcalf Bottoms. They were Hettie, Margaret, Louisa, Polly, and Martha.

Q. Did any of them get married?

A. Two of the sisters got engaged, but both

The Walker family home in the 1930s.

men died in accidents. These five sisters remained spinsters. Caroline, the youngest Walker daughter, was the only sister who got married—she married Jim Shelton, who worked with lumber companies and photographed the lumber industry and also made many family photos. None of the Walker Sisters drove, but Jim Shelton would take them places and get them supplies.

Q. Why did they get to stay in the park?

A. As other people moved out of the park in the 1930s, the Walker sisters made no plans to move and did not respond to offers to sell their land or to threats of forced sale. Visitors to the park started visiting the sisters to see their beautiful coverlets and their

---

The Walker cabin had no closets. Clothes, baskets, tools, kitchen utensils, and just about everything else, hung from pegs on the rafters.

self-reliant lifestyle. By 1940, park officials were in an awkward position—the Walker Sisters ignored all offers, and there was no way they could drag these five old women off their land without bad publicity. The Sisters resolved the issue by turning the tables on the park service with a "take it or leave it" offer to sell their buildings and 122 acres with a lifetime lease.

Q. The Walker homestead had many outbuildings—a barn, a corn crib, and apple barn, a spring house to keep milk and butter cold, a smoke house, and a tub mill. Did they have an outhouse?
A. No. Margaret Jane said she didn't like the smell of an outhouse, so men used the hills above the house and women below.

Q. How did the five sisters live after their parents died and the other siblings moved away?
A. Before the park, their male relatives would come and do the heavy work—plowing, storing wood for the winter, hog killing. A couple of the sisters worked outside the park for short periods, one in Knoxville. Later, the sisters became self-sufficient, getting some income by selling souvenirs and honey to park visitors. They ordered cloth and seeds and fancy hats from catalogs.

Q. How did they get medicine?
A. Margaret Jane Walker raised eleven children to adulthood with her skills of herbal medicine, and she taught her children how to grow and prepare remedies.

Q. What are limbertwig, Milam, Buckingham, Sour John, and Abraham?
A. Just some of the kinds of apples the Walker Sisters grew in their orchard.

Q. In 1946 the Saturday Evening Post published an article "Time Stood Still in the Smokies" about the Walker Sisters with many photographs. How did the sisters react to the article?
A. They cracked up. They laughed and laughed at the way the magazine readers saw them. And of course they got many more visitors after that.

Log cabin dwellers used newspaper for wallpaper.

Pi Beta Phi, the first women's fraternity of Monmouth College, Ohio, started a settlement school in Gatlinburg. The women taught the basics and also health and crafts. They encouraged a revival of old skills such as weaving and basket-making, and helped people make crafts that tourists would buy. The elementary school was later taken over by Sevier County, but the arts and crafts part became Arrowmont School, affiliated with the University of Tennessee.

Classes in the modern Pi Beta Phi school participate frequently in the Parks as Classrooms program.

Q. What are Bonaparte's March, Cat's Trails, and Snail's Trails?
A. A few of the coverlet weave patterns that the Walker sisters used. They sheared the sheep, carded the wool, spun it, and dyed it with walnut, poke, and other natural dyes, and wove the beautiful patterns passed down in the family from Scotland. Sometimes they combined wool with cotton thread to make linsey-woolsey. They also made traditional quilts, using batting from their own cotton but possibly store-bought brightly colored cloth.

Q. How long did the Walker Sisters stay in the park?
A. Through the 1950s. By the late forties, even though they had become so popular with park visitors, they felt they were too old to keep welcoming them, so they asked the park to remove signs to their house. The last spinster sister, Louisa, died in 1964. Caroline died in 1966.

Q. What happened to their cabin?
A. It's still there, in Greenbrier Cove, a two-mile hike from Metcalf Bottoms. The park maintains it as the sisters left it, so you can visit it and imagine living there.

Q. What happened to their belongings?
A. The park has catalogued and stored all their clothes, quilts, coverlets, tools, kitchenware, furniture, looms, powder horns, treadle sewing machine, cushions, dolls, and knickknacks. When funds are available, these will be displayed, and records of these artifacts can be found in many books. The sun bonnets are particularly interesting.

The Pi Beta Phi Fraternity for Women started with 12 members in 1867. The Gatlinburg Settlement School was its first philanthropic venture in 1912.

Q. How did they get all that stuff?

A. Hairy John was a skilled blacksmith, leatherworker, and carpenter. When Margaret Jane's parents died, he took their log house apart and joined it to the two-story Walker cabin. He built chairs, tables, beds, harnesses, a cotton gin, an ash hopper, everything. So the Walker Sisters were using 19th-century tools and skills as 20th-century visitors came to watch.

Q. What's an ash hopper?

A. A wooden funnel used to make lye from ashes. Water running through the ashes is collected and the resulting lye water is boiled until it is strong enough to dissolve a feather (don't try this at home). Then beef fat or lard is mixed with the lye to make soap.

Q. Who was Black Bill Walker?

A. A settler in Walker Valley, or what is now Tremont. Black Bill had three wives and 27 children. When he married his second wife, Mary Anne Moore, her brother traveled up from Georgia to rescue her from a situation that he disapproved of, but he liked Walker Valley so much that he stayed and married one of Bill Walker's daughters. Bill Walker then married Moll. The first two wives mid-wifed Moll's children, and each wife had a cabin of her own. (Black Bill Walker and Hairy John Walker were double first cousins.)

Q. How did Bill Walker support such a large family?

A. He sold cattle and probably several tons of honey from his bee hives, which were made from hollow sections of black gum trees. He trapped or shot bears, beavers, otters, and raccoons to sell the pelts.

Q. Where did the children go to school?

One unit of the Confederate Army, the 69th N.C., was made up of Cherokees and led by Will Thomas. They may have kept a few raiders and bushwhackers out, and they did a fair amount of raiding.

A. In 1902 Bill Walker helped establish a teacherage, a small building where a teacher lived, taught (mostly Bill's kids), and preached on Sunday. Later they showed movies at the teacherage on Saturday nights, and it became known as the building of education, damnation, and salvation.

> Bill Walker loved **Walker Valley** and sold it to Colonel Townsend's Little River Lumber Company only with a promise that they wouldn't log the virgin timber on Thunderhead Prong. Townsend kept the promise as long as he lived, but after he died, the timber was cut.
>
> **Colonel Townsend** gave some land on the Middle Prong of the Little River for a Girl Scout camp, Camp Mary Townsend. That camp is now the Great Smoky Mountains Institute (GSMIT), a residential environmental education facility. Hundreds of school classes have spent a week there—some teachers bring their fifth graders every year, without fail—even in blizzards. They also have environmental summer camp and teacher training programs.

Q. What was the staple crop that supported Smokies settlers?
 A) Wheat   B) Corn   C) Potatoes
A. B) Corn was the easiest crop to grow on rocky slopes; it was easy to store, provided bread, pone, mush, and liquor.

Q. How did settlers grind the corn?
A. Before the Civil War, families had tub mills, small wooden structures that could grind a family's supply. After the war, larger grist mills served communities and became social centers.

Q. Where can we see tub mills?
A. Along the Roaring Fork Motor Nature Trail and at the Bud Ogle place on Cherokee Orchard Road. The Ancient Greeks had tub mills with pretty much the same design.

Tub mill

Millers kept one-eighth of each bushel of corn or wheat that they ground as a toll. Why do you suppose that some millers got the nickname "Dusty"?

Q. How about gristmills?

A. Two restored grist mills operate in the park, Cable Mill in Cades Cove (with an overshot wooden wheel) and Mingus Mill near Oconaluftee (with a metal turbine). You can watch a miller work, and you can even get some fresh corn meal. When the mills were first built, all the gears were made of wood, often apple wood, and greased with beef tallow.

Q. What do these mountain settlement terms mean?
Puncheon
Granny hole
Shake
Fittified Spring
Tub mill
Weaner house

A. **Puncheon**—a log that has been split so that it has a flat surface. Floors and benches were made of puncheon logs before sawn logs were available.

Granny hole—a small window near the fireplace of a log cabin. The oldest family member could sit near the fire and still see out, or could have enough light for needle work. Often it was the only window in a cabin and could be shuttered.

Shake—a shingle made by splitting wood, usually oak, with a froe knife.

Fittified spring—a spring that has fits and starts instead of a steady flow.

Tub mill—a small outbuilding over a creek with the current directed to turn a wheel to grind corn. Usually for one or two families.

Weaner house—when a young couple got married, they'd build a cabin on their parents' property until they could get their own land.

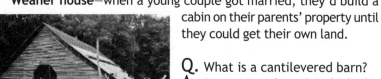

Drovers barn, Mountain Farm Museum

Q. What is a cantilevered barn?
A. A two-story barn in which the upper story, or loft, extends beyond both long sides from the first story. Cattle and equipment can be sheltered under the overhangs. An

Corn and wheat were ground between two millstones. The upper one rotates. The miller can adjust the fineness by raising or lowering the upper stone.

architectural study in 1980 found six cantilevered barns in Virginia, three in North Carolina, and 316 in East Tennessee, mostly in Blount and Sevier counties.

Q. Where can we see cantilevered barns?
A. Cable Mill and Tipton Homeplace in Cades Cove, Smoky Mountain Heritage Center in Townsend, Messer Barn in Greenbrier, and outside the park in Tennessee. Modern architects have used the plan; most notably, Maya Lin (the designer of the Vietnam Memorial in Washington, DC) used it for the Alex Haley Library in Norris, Tennessee.

Q. Where are the best places to see other historic buildings in the park?
A. Cades Cove, Cataloochee, Roaring Fork Motor Nature Trail, and the Mountain Farm Museum near the Oconaluftee Visitor Center. The Noah "Bud" Ogle homestead on Cherokee Orchard Road is a great place to imagine what life was like back then.

> Early park planners chose to preserve only log cabins and structures that were built before 1890, so as you tour historic sites keep in mind that many areas, especially Cades Cove, Cataloochee, and Hazel Creek had 20th-century buildings that were not preserved. Unfortunately, none of the pioneer stores was preserved.

Q. Why so many preserved buildings?
A. From the beginning, park administrators decided to preserve buildings as examples of a way of life that developed in these mountains and a tribute to people who, willingly or unwillingly, sacrificed their land and way of life for the park. The park preserves the largest collection of log structures in the world.

> People who had small summer homes in **Elkmont** requested life leases to about 70 cabins, a large clubhouse, and the Wonderland Hotel. They managed to renew the leases in the 1970s, but finally abandoned them amid much controversy in the 1990s. The buildings are falling down; the park has plans to restore some with historic value. You can walk around this vacation community, but the buildings are off limits.

If you see daffodils on a Smokies hike, you are almost certainly walking through a former home site where daffodil bulbs were planted.

Q. Where is the Moonshine Capital of the World?

A. Well, several places might compete for that honor, but Cocke County, Tennessee, has to be a strong contender. Many of Cocke County's stills were in the Cosby area of the GSMNP, under cover of rhododendron.

Q. Where did the tradition and skills of moonshine whiskey come from?

A. People in Scotland and Ireland operated stills in the 1300s, probably earlier. George Washington had a nice still at Mount Vernon. When Scots-Irish immigrants moved down from Pennsylvania and Virginia, they brought the tradition and probably some of the equipment.

Q. How did George Washington contribute to the art of making moonshine whiskey?

A. He levied an excise tax on alcohol to help pay debts from the Revolutionary War. Making your own whiskey wasn't much different from making your own soap, but suddenly, folks who could hide their stills could sell the product without paying taxes. It was better business than lugging corn to the market. The tax was repealed a few years later, but reestablished in 1862. Same reason, different war.

Revenuers after a raid

Q. Most of the moonshine liquor was transported out of the mountains to be sold. But, since it was illegal, how would you buy some fresh from the source?

A. Since revenuers (tax collectors for the IRS) would often try sting operations (in fact, there are stories of revenuers getting drunk and being brought around by the moonshiners' families), here's the selling system that developed: While walking along a pretty mountain

---

Moonshine whiskey looks like water. Experts can estimate the proof by observing the bead (bubbles) that forms when shaken.

trail you might come to a bell hanging on a tree. You ring it and put a few dollars in a box. Then continue hiking. On your way back, if you passed the secret inspection, your Mason jar of moonshine will be waiting for you.

Q. How did moonshiners know when revenuers were planning a raid?
A. People living along the entrance road to all parts of the mountains had signals—maybe a hunting horn or owl call. The folks back at the still had plenty of time to disappear. Often the most success revenuers could have was smashing the stills.

Q. What other boosts did the moonshine business get over the years?
A. In 1890, because of a depression, the alcohol tax was increased. Then, Tennessee and North Carolina "went dry" by passing state prohibition laws, and in 1920, prohibition became the law of the whole nation. Another boost, of course, was cars! Moonshiners could sell their products in Knoxville, Asheville, and beyond. Battles erupted among moonshiners, revenuers, and other interested parties, such as the Ku Klux Klan.

Q. How long did Prohibition last?
   A) 6 months   B) 8 years   C) 13 years
A. C) 13 years

Q. Who were the Blockaders?
A. Revenuers would set up blockades on the roads out of mountains valleys, so the moonshiners responded by souping up their cars to smash through the blockades or to evade pursuers. "The Ballad of Thunder Road" is about a chase from the mountains through West Knoxville that ended in a fiery crash, fuelled by gas and moonshine. Robert Mitchum starred in the 1957 movie *Thunder Road* and later recorded the ballad.
   Here's the chorus:
And there was thunder, thunder, over Thunder Road
Thunder was his engine, and white lightning was his load
There was moonshine, moonshine to quench the Devil's thirst
The Law they swore they'd get him, but the Devil got him first.

Remedy for snakebite, reported in a Foxfire *magazine: Drink whiskey and also apply it to the bite.*

Q. What other business came from these conflicts?
A. NASCAR! Some Blockaders in North Georgia set up racing courses for their cars and charged admission...and the rest is the history of a national sport. The first NASCAR drivers didn't give up their night jobs, though.

Q. What do you need to run a still?
A. Some grain, usually corn, clean cold water, some barrels and pipes, a worm (a coiled copper tube).

Q. How does a still work?
A. **Fermentation**—yeast cells break down starch or sugar to form alcohol (ethanol).
Heating. This part involved a wood fire; revenuers might be stationed on the ridge to watch for smoke. So, do it at night.
Distillation—alcohol boils at a lower temperature than water, so the two can be separated when the fermented mash is heated...just right.
Condensation—the alcohol steam is cooled by sending it through the worm, which is immersed in cool creek water in the worm box. The condensed liquid moonshine alcohol drips into a bucket and gets whisked into Mason jars.

Q. How strong is moonshine?
A. That depends on the skill and honesty of the distiller, but usually 100 proof, or 50% ethanol. (For comparison, the alcohol content of wine is 10-15%, and for beer 5-8%.) Careless distilling or contaminants from the pipes could make the stuff poisonous.

Q. How much corn is needed to make one gallon of whiskey?

    A) Three bushels   B) Four bushels
    C) Five bushels
A. A) Three bushels.

Q. What is it called when a moonshiner saves out some mash from one batch and pours it into the next batch to make the fermentation faster?
A. Sour mash.

The warm liquid in the mash was called beer and had some alcohol; still workers needing refreshment would insert a hollow stem or quill to get a drink.

Q. Why did some folks sprout the corn before grinding it?

A. When the corn kernels sprout, starch changes to sugar, which speeds the fermentation. The kernels have been malted (sprouted and then dried), so it becomes malt liquor.

Q. Popcorn Sutton, one of the last oldtime moonshiners, wrote an autobiography called *Me and My Likker*. He died in 2009, at age 61, possibly by suicide to avoid a prison term for having 850 gallons of white lightning, mash, loaded guns, and lots more. How did Popcorn get caught?

Sutton and portable still

A. One of his three stills exploded, and the fire department came.

Quill Rose, described by Horace Kephart in *Our Southern Highlanders*, was only caught once. When asked in court if he ever aged his whiskey, he replied that he had kept some for a week once but didn't notice any difference in the taste.

"Knoxville, Jan. 28. The people living in the mountains...have acquired something of a national reputation...by their persistent defiance of internal revenue laws. To spite the law and in spite of the espionage exercised over them by the officers, they have gone on making illicit whiskey in their mountain fastnesses."—*New York Times*, 1880. The article goes on to describe a packed courtroom where the judge had offered amnesty—if the moonshiners would plead guilty, their records would be cleared. Hundreds of moonshiners came to Knoxville for the amnesty and then melted back into the mountains to get on with their distilling.

Moonshiners had to protect their stills from revenuers and also from wild hogs, which could break into the barrel and slurp up the hot mash.

Q. Many of the geographical names in the park (Porters Flats, Gregory Bald) are for European settlers who lived there. Some (Otter Creek, Chestnut Branch) are named for plants or animals. What are the following named for?

Pigeon and Little Pigeon Rivers
A. Passenger pigeons, once traveling in huge flocks, now extinct.

Mount Chapman, Davis Ridge, Campbell Overlook, Morton Overlook
A. Members of the Tennessee Park Commission who worked to promote the national park.

Mount Kephart, Masa Knob, Mount Ambler, Mount Weaver, Mount Squires, Webb Creek
A. North Carolina park founders

Mellinger Death Ridge, near Cades Cove
A. Jasper Mellinger fell into an illegal bear trap. The owners of the trap found him still alive and killed him to avoid getting caught. The stories vary; either one of the killers confessed on his death bed or someone found Mellinger's body years later and recognized his wrist watch.

More Liquor Branch
A. A creek near Cades Cove...hmmm.

Bone Valley
A. Farmers used to drive their cattle up to grassy balds in spring to graze. In 1888, a late blizzard trapped the cows on Spence and Russell fields. Cow bones littered the head of Bone Valley for decades.

Huggins Hell
A. A hell is a tangle of laurel and rhododendron and greenbrier, usually on a steep slope. One version of the story is that Irving Huggins entered the hell on the side of Mount Le Conte

There's one record of a steer that became very fat on mash when he became a repeat visitor to a still.

and emerged a week later, nearly dead. The creek coming out of Huggins Hell is Styx Branch. Hikers are advised to stay on trails.

Injun Creek
A. A creek in Greenbrier named for the steam boiler (engine, pronounced locally as "injun") that fell into it from a logging railroad; the "injun" still lies there rusting.

Bloody Branch
A. A tributary of Meigs Creek in a very steep valley. William Walker once went out searching for his pigs, which had been set loose in the woods to fatten up on chestnuts and beechnuts. It seemed like too much work to drive them home, so he slaughtered them on the spot and rinsed them in the creek.

Boogerman Trail
A. Robert Palmer, when at school in Cataloochee Valley, was asked what he wanted to be when he grew up. "The Boogerman," he is said to have answered. When he grew up and owned 250 acres of virgin forest, he drove lumbermen away. Because of his temper, we can walk through beautiful virgin forest on the Boogerman Trail, a favorite Halloween hike.

Boogerman's brother was called Turkey George Palmer. He set a high-walled trap for turkeys on the theory that if he could drive the turkeys into the trap they couldn't get airborne. It worked fine until Turkey George jumped in to catch himself a turkey and the other turkeys beat him up with their wings and feet.

And while we're telling stories about Turkey George...he claimed to have killed 105 bears, and requested that he be buried in a steel coffin so that the bears wouldn't dig him up in revenge.

Booger Palmer sold his land to the Park Commission
for $5,375 in 1929.

Curry He and Curry She Mountains
A. Two small mountains near Metcalf Bottoms, named for a misunderstanding. A Cherokee word, *gurahi*, refers to an edible plant that grows there; the settlers hearing this thought that if there was a gura he there ought to be a gura she.

Bote Mountain
A. The story is that Dr. James Anderson, President of Maryville College, wanted to build a road to Spence Field. He asked Cherokees on his work crew to vote on the route. Not having a "v" sound in Cherokee, they "boted" for this ridge; the other ridge in the running became "Defeat Ridge."

Brakeshoe Spring
A. A train engineer jammed a brakeshoe, long curved piece of metal, between rocks in a creek so that it created a spout of water where he could lean out of his engine to drink as the train passed by. The brakeshoe remained in service until sometime in the 1970s.

Q. What was the Oconaluftee Turnpike?
A. The main route over the Smokies from North Carolina to Tennessee before the Newfound Gap Road was built in the 1930s. It crossed the state line at Indian Gap, two miles west of Newfound Gap. Like the Cataloochee Turnpike, it was built by local residents and charged tolls.

Q. How much toll would you have paid in 1850 to ride your horse on the turnpike?
A. 6 1/4 cents; other fares were 2 cents for each cow, 1 cent for a pig, and 75 cents for a 4-wheeled carriage full of tourists.

Q. How many cemeteries are there in the Smokies?
A. 170 documented ones. Many consist of just a couple graves; one near the base of Greenbrier Pinnacle has three small stones—one for an 8-year-old girl and two for 2-year-old girls.

Q. Where is the largest park cemetery?
A. In Greenbrier, with 750 graves.

In 2009, park rangers used ground-penetrating radar to search for unmarked graves so that they can be protected.

Q. Which denominations built churches in the early 1800s?
A. Baptists and Methodists. Methodist ministers were ordained circuit riders, circulating among several churches. In remote communities, marrying, burying, and baptizing all had to wait until spring. Baptist ministers came from the communities and usually were farmers or people with other jobs.

Q. What's the difference between a Primitive Baptist church and a Missionary Baptist church?

A. The early Baptist church had disagreements about their role in the community. The Missionary Baptists favored Sunday school, temperance societies, and other missions; the Primitive Baptists felt that there was no scriptural basis for these activities. Later, the Methodist churches split over the issue of slavery, so for a while there were four congregations in Cades Cove.

Missionary Baptist Church (1894)

Q. How many churches are preserved by the National Park Service in Cades Cove?
A. Three.

Q. What is Decoration Day?
A. On the last Sunday in May, people join together to clean the graves and then have a meal on the church grounds. In Cades Cove, all families forgot their differences and went to all four churches on Decoration Day. Decoration Day is still observed in the Smokies—people come into the park to honor their relatives who once lived here. On Decoration Days, the park provides transportation and access to closed areas such as Little Cataloochee.

Q. Who was the first Methodist circuit rider?
A. Bishop Francis Asbury in 1810. He rode his horse into Cataloochee on a rainy November day, crossing swollen creeks and steep ridges. His diary comment was "What an awful day." You can

When someone died in Cataloochee or Cades Cove, the church bell would toll and then pause, and then ring the number of years the victim had lived.

retrace his path on Asbury Trail (which was also an old Cherokee trail) but choose better weather.

Q. What popular Christmas song refers to circuit riders?
A. "Winter Wonderland." Remember the verse:
In the meadow we will build a snowman,
And we'll say that he is Parson Brown,
He'll say, "Are you married?" We'll say "No, man,
But you can do the job when you're in town."
This verse and another were changed by some singers in the 1950s because it was too suggestive; Parson Brown became a circus clown instead.

A circuit riding minister called **Old Dry Frye** appears in many mountain folk tales. It seems Old Dry Frye loved fried chicken so much that he choked on a chicken bone. His horrified hosts hustled the body into someone else's hen house; the hen owners heard the commotion, found the body, and thought Old Dry Frye had died on their property...the body gets transferred to several houses in the community until someone ties Old Dry Frye onto a horse...and you can still see Old Dry Frye on the horse on foggy evenings, searching for more fried chicken.

Q. What is a "shivaree?"
A. When a young couple gets married, a crowd shows up after the festivities with guns, trumpets, bells, and fireworks. Then they drag the couple out of bed and keep them apart all night. They may ride the groom around on a rail and his bride in a tub.

Q. Sugarlands Valley was named for the maple sugar that settlers made. Why did they stop making maple sugar?
A. Maple wood was good for furniture-making, and selective logging in the 1880s and 90s took the biggest sugar maple trees. Also, after the Civil War, sorghum became available and yielded more syrup.

Sorghum

Most people would know who had been sick lately and know who had died. The local coffin maker would probably know what size coffin to make without asking.

Q. Why did logging speed up so suddenly after 1900?

A. The arrival of railroads and steam engines, which made it easier to get the timber out of the mountains and also to send it to distant markets. Also, companies had exhausted timber supplies in New England and the upper Midwest.

Q. What do the following logging terms mean?
Doogaloo
Misery whip
Stringtown
Peavey

A. **Doogaloo**: Coins minted by the logging companies to be used in the stores. Remember *Sixteen Tons,* the song that said, "I owe my soul to the Company Store"? In coal mining areas, this money was called scrip.

Misery whip: A long two-man saw used on large trees.

Stringtown: A row of houses for the lumber workers. Each house could be picked up by a logging crane and set on a rail car for transport to the next logging area.

Peavey: A hook on the end of a long spiked pole that was used to turn logs. The logger would spike the pole and then engage the hook. This was dangerous work—sometimes logs would shift and crush workers. It was also used to keep logs moving in splash dams. It was invented by Joseph Peavey of Stillwater, Maine.

Q. About how much of the present park was logged?

A. Two-thirds.

Steam engines carried the logs out of the Smokies (some logs were bigger than the traincar itself), but they also carried tourists in. Many of these tourists, such as Paul Fink and Harvey Broome of Tennessee, became persuasive park advocates.

Q. When did logging end in the Smokies?

A. The last tree was cut and sent to the saw mill in Townsend on July 6, 1939.

For a fictional account of the conflict between lumber companies and park advocates, read Serena *by Ron Rash (2008). Horace Kephart appears as a fictional character.*

"When I first came into the Smokies the whole region was one superb forest primeval...The vast trees met overhead like cathedral roofs....Not long ago I went to that same place again. It was wrecked, ruined, desecrated, turned into a thousand rubbish heaps, utterly vile and mean...Did anyone ever thank God for a lumberman's slashing?" Horace Kephart, 1923, on observing logged areas

Q. How did the first Model-T cars get to Elkmont?
A. On the logging railroads—they had rail wheels instead of tires.

You can still see rusted cables and rails along some creeks that were logged. And some trail switchbacks still show a long straight stretch where an engine could reverse.

Geology and Geography

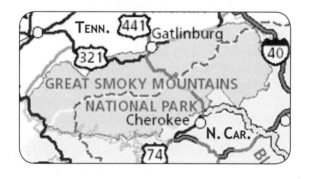

Q. How big is the Great Smoky Mountains National Park?
A. About 800 square miles (2072 sq. km). The park would fit twice into Rhode Island, the smallest of the United States. In acres, it's about half a million.

Q. What are the dimensions of the park?
A. The park is about 55 miles (88 km) long and about 20 miles (32 km) wide. It is shaped like a potato with a rectangular piece cut out of the southeastern side.

Q. What is that rectangular piece?
A. It is part of Qualla Boundary, the home of the Eastern Band of the Cherokee Indians which includes the town of Cherokee.

Q. So it's their reservation?
A. No, it's not a reservation. A reservation is land that the U.S. Government set aside for Indian groups. Qualla Boundary is land that Cherokees owned or bought for themselves after the Civil War and still own today.

Q. What is the Cherokee name for the Smokies?
A. Shaconage, or Place of Blue Smoke.

Q. What is the highest point in the Smokies?
A. Clingmans Dome, at 6643 feet (2025 meters).

Q. How many Smokies peaks are above treeline?
A. None. Clingmans Dome would have to be 1,000 feet higher to have a treeline like the one on Mount Washington in New Hampshire.

Q. So New Hampshire has higher mountains than the Smokies?
A. No, Mount Washington is only 6288 feet (1917 meters). But since it is farther north, the treeline is lower.

Q. Are there mountains in the eastern U.S. higher than Clingmans Dome?
A. Two, Mount Mitchell, 6684 feet (2037 m), and Mount Craig, 6647 feet (2026 m), both in North Carolina, but outside the Smokies. (Well, really, according to some folks, Mount Craig is just a sub-peak of Mount Mitchell.)

Q. Who was Clingman?
A. Thomas Lanier Clingman was a Civil War general and later a U.S. senator. He argued that the southern mountains were higher than New England mountains, but northerners wouldn't allow such ridiculous ideas until the Swiss geographer Arnold Guyot came with sophisticated measuring instruments and proved Clingman right in 1858.

The boulders at the Clingmans Dome parking lot were formed 800-545 million years ago. They were pushed up 300 million years ago.

Q. How did they measure elevation above sea level back then?
A. Guyot used large glass barometers and thermometers and measured the change in atmospheric pressure and temperature as he climbed. He needed donkeys to carry the equipment and guides to show him the way because there were no trails. If the weather changed during his climb he had to go back down and start over again. One small mountain is called Thermo Knob because Guyot (or the donkey) broke a valuable thermometer there.

Q. If they named the Clingmans Dome after him, why isn't it written Clingman's Dome? Did your proofreader mess up?
A. The U.S. Geological Survey (established in 1879) makes maps and certifies the official names of places. The USGS does not use apostrophes in place names. Did you notice that they also don't use commas in elevations on maps (6643 feet instead of 6,643)?

Q. How many peaks in the Smokies are over 6000 feet (1800 m)?
   A) 8   B) 14   C) 20
A. C) 20. The three highest are Clingmans, 6643 feet; Guyot, 6621 feet; and Le Conte High Top, 6593. You can add a rock to the pile on High Top to make Le Conte the winner, but freeze-thaw erosion flattens the pile each winter.

Mount Le Conte

Q. As you drive through Pigeon Forge toward the Smokies you can see a large mountain ahead with three peaks. What mountain is it?
   A) Clingmans Dome   B) Mount Le Conte   C) Mount Guyot
A. C) Mount Le Conte. The view is best at the turn for Dolly-wood.

You can get a geologic map at the visitor centers.

Q. Where is the lowest elevation of the Smokies?
A. At the mouth of Abrams Creek, 840 feet (256 m).

Q. What is the longest river in the park?
A. The Little River, of course! And its tributaries flowing off Clingmans Dome and Mount Collins are Spud Town, Rattler, Snake Tongue, and Devil creeks. Spend some time up there (Campsite 30 on Little River Trail) if you dare.

Q. Where does water from the Smokies end up?
　　A) Atlantic Ocean　　B) Gulf of Mexico　　C) Both
A. B) Gulf of Mexico, a small part of the Atlantic Ocean. And it has to go to Kentucky get there. All Smokies creeks and rivers (even the ones in North Carolina) flow into the Tennessee River, which goes down to Chattanooga and then swings north by Nashville and joins the Ohio at Paducah, Kentucky. The Ohio drains into the Mississippi River, which goes to the Gulf.

Q. How many natural lakes are there in the Smokies?
A. None. Water in the park is always flowing, except for a few seasonal ponds or swampy areas.

Q. What National Forests border on the Smokies?
A. Cherokee National Forest in Tennessee, Nantahala and Pisgah national forests of North Carolina.

Q. Advalorem is the name of a:
　　A) Creek near Clingmans Dome
　　B) Cherokee Chief
　　C) Gatlinburg PR firm that promotes tourism
　　D) Licensed moonshine still
A. A) Creek near Clingmans Dome.

Q. What is the annual rainfall of the Smokies?
A. 55-85 inches (140 cm-215 cm), more at higher elevations. The record for rainfall measured at Mount Le Conte was in 2009 at 104 inches (264 cm).

Mesozoic rocks, which might contain dinosaur fossils, don't exist in the Smokies.

Q. Why more at higher elevations?
A. Most air currents come from the west. As air gets pushed up to higher elevation, it cools. Colder air holds less water, which then falls as rain or snow. On December 22, 2009, Newfound Gap got 20 inches (50 cm) of snow and Mount Le Conte (1500 feet higher) got 32 inches (80 cm).

Q. How much cooler is it on the mountain tops than in Cherokee or Gatlinburg?
A. It can be 20 or more degrees F cooler at Clingmans Dome. Many people are unprepared for Clingmans Dome weather—they

enter the park in shorts and get out of the car to find wind, cold rain, fog. Have extra clothes with you. It can snow at high elevations in May. The temperature decreases approximately 3 degrees F for each 1000 feet of elevation gain.

Q. What is hoar frost?
A. One of the best things about hiking in winter. Ice crystals form when water-saturated air or fog goes below the freezing point of water. The ice forms on twigs or needles or fern fronds as sharp crystals or patterns. If there's wind, the crystals will grow horizontally, from every available surface (you, too, if you stand still long enough). Then, if the sun comes out, the whole scene sparkles. Later you'll hear tinkling and crashing as the hoar frost, also called rime, falls off.

Q. Where's the best place to see hoar frost?
A. At high elevation. Sometimes from Knoxville or other distant views the mountains look white but it hasn't snowed recently— that's the time to drive up to look at hoar frost.

Q. What are ice flowers?
A. Also called ice needles. During the first cold weather of the fall, water in the soil freezes and extrudes from holes in the soil like toothpaste coming out of a hundred tiny tubes. The ice needles may get several inches long and stand there until knocked over. Ice flowers also form on the stems of some plants, and the ice forms swirly patterns as the water in the stem freezes and expands.

People used to mine Epsom salts from Alum Cave Bluff.

Q. Which mountains are older—the Smokies or the Rockies?
A. The Smokies by far—they were pushed up between 400 and 300 million years ago by a continental collision with Africa. The Appalachian Mountains, which include the Smokies, are the oldest mountains in the world.

Q. How long did the collision with Africa take?
A. Several million years—not a hit-and-run. The tectonic plates of what we now call North America and Africa ground together, causing earthquakes, uplifts, and probably some pyrotechnics. The extreme heat and pressure hardened sandstone and melted some of it that later became crystals or quartzite. Shale became harder slate.

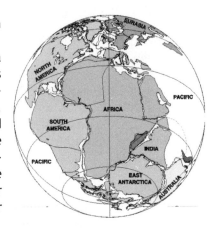

Q. Where can we see evidence of these changes?
A. The rocks that were blasted to form the Newfound Gap parking lot show lines (strata) that were once horizontal (from sedimentation) but are now slanted, curved, or broken. At spots on the Appalachian Trail just south of Clingmans Dome, you can see an overthrust fault—as Africa pushed the rocks northwest, some of them tipped up until they broke. You can see the jagged edges, and the other parts lying down in the woods on the Tennessee side. Imagine a bulldozer pushing at pavement until it buckles and breaks. Then imagine that the pavement is nine miles thick as you look out at the waves and waves of mountains in the views from Clingmans Dome. Look for similar evidence on road cuts along the Newfound Gap Road and at Alum Cave Bluff.

Q. Wow. What made Africa do that?
A. Plate tectonics. The continents of the earth's crust float on molten magma, and changes in heat and pressure way down there affect the land surface. Watch out—the African tectonic plate may come back some day.

The tectonic collision with Africa created the entire Appalachian chain, from Newfoundland in Canada to Alabama.

Q. Why aren't the Appalachians higher, then?

A. They once were—maybe three times higher. (And they might get that high again if Africa does come back, but don't hold your breath.) Heavy rainfall and freezing and thawing cause erosion—about one or two inches per thousand years. You do the math.

Some rocks are harder than others, and the mountains contain an amazing mixture of different rock types. Water causes features such as waterfalls, bluffs, and crags by eroding the softer rocks faster.

> Some evidence of the power of water isn't so ancient. In 1993 a cloudburst near the top of Le Conte started a flash flood and landslide that scoured a creek that crosses the trail. Boulders rolled and huge trees hurtled down with the flood. Hikers were on both sides of the creek, but fortunately no one was crossing the creek just then.

> The Appalachian **orogeny** (mountain building) occurred over several collisions between the African and North American plates. The building, or uplift, of the Appalachians ended with the construction of the supercontinent Pangea, at which time the Appalachians were much longer. Pieces of the rocks and minerals of this chain occur in Morocco (the Anti-Atlas Mountains) and Scotland.
>
> The Cherokee version of mountain orogeny: The People and animals lived on a platform suspended above the water. When it got too crowded, they sent Water Beetle down to find land. She dove and brought back mud, but it was too wet, so they sent Turkey Vulture down to dry it out. When he got tired, his wings dipped and tossed up waves of the mud to form the mountains. Then they needed light, which was on the other side of the world. Mole dug a tunnel, but couldn't bring back a piece of the sun, so Grandmother Spider made the long journey and brought back a piece of the sun wrapped in her web.
>
> For more on Cherokee creation stories, read *Sacred Formulas and Myths of the Cherokee* by James Mooney, 1890.

Granite, schist, and gneiss occur in the North Carolina half of the park and in other North Carolina mountains, but are rare in Tennessee.

Q. Did glaciers ever cover the Smokies?
A. No, but the glaciers affected the biology of the Smokies. Ice covered large areas north of the Ohio River. Plants and animals displaced by the glaciers found refuge in Smokies valleys, even when the Smokies peaks iced over each winter.

Q. When did the last glaciers recede?
A) 10,000 years ago   B) 100,000 years ago
C) 1,000,000 years ago
A. A) 10,000 year ago

Q. How long did the last Ice Age, known as the Wisconsin Ice Age, last?
A) 20,000 years   B) 200,000 years
C) 2,000,000 years
A. C) 2,000,000 years

The rock of the Smokies is mostly the Ocoee Superseries of rock, formed between 900 and 600 million years ago. Ocoee (pronounced *oh-KOH-ee*) is the Cherokee name for wild apricot, Tennessee's state wildflower, and the Ocoee Super-series are late Precambrian rock formations of sandstone, siltstone, phyllite, and slate. This rock was pushed up over fossil-bearing Ordovician limestones formed between 600 and 300 million years ago.

Q. What is the highest mountain in the eastern U.S. with no road or trail to the summit?
A. Mount Guyot, at 6621 feet (2018 m) on the Smokies crest east of Newfound Gap. The Appalachian Trail goes within half a mile of the summit of Mount Guyot.

Q. What famous geographer contributed to the theory of glacia-tion, or the Ice Ages?
A. Arnold Guyot, working with Louis Agassiz, a Harvard biologist. Guyot also has three other mountains, a crater, and a glacier named after him.

Q. What is a limestone window?

The bedrock of Cades Cove is limestone and dolomite and contains a few fossils of shellfish and arthropods.

A. A place where the ancient rocks have been eroded away to expose the younger limestone underneath, probably because of thinner layers or cracks that allowed the erosion. Cades Cove, Wears Valley, Tuckaleechee Cove (with its great limestone caves) are examples of limestone windows.

Q. What are boulder fields?

A. During the Ice Ages, mountaintops probably had ice caps, and as that ice thawed and refroze, it cracked the bed rock and sent chunks hurtling down. In some places, they even look like a river of boulders. Look for them on Roaring Fork Motor Nature Trail, Trillium Gap Trail above Grotto Falls, Huskey Gap Trail, Laurel Falls Trail, and more.

> Trees can't grow on the boulders, so they are a wonderful habitat for mosses, ferns, and wildflowers that get established in pockets of soil. Crevices between the boulders provide animal homes.

Q. Where are the Dolly Parton Peaks?

A. Near Little Duck Hawk Ridge. You can see them from Inspiration Point and Alum Cave Bluffs.

Dolly Parton Peaks

Q. Nearly a billion years ago, the rocks that now make up the Smokies were deposited by erosion from even earlier mountains onto an ancient seabed. What is the name of that ancient ocean?

A. Iapetus Ocean, a precursor to the Atlantic. It was named for the father of Atlas in Greek mythology.

Q. So the rocks of the Smokies are sedimentary?

A. Yes, originally, but the process of continental collision lifted, pushed, crushed, fractured, melted, and mixed them. In other words, they became metamorphic, or changed.

Q. At Clingmans Dome, Mount Cammerer, and many other places, you can see veins of white quartz. How did they form?

More mountains on the Tennessee side face north, and they were affected more by the Ice Ages. Most of the boulder fields are in Tennessee.

A. Under extreme pressure, hot water dissolved minerals and rushed through cracks in the sandstone. As the cracks cooled, the glassy quartz hardened.

Often you'll see big chunks of quartz on the trail or in creeks. There's one as big as a sofa on the Appalachian Trail at the intersection of Sugarland Mountain Trail. Quartz is harder than Thunderhead Sandstone, so the veins may stick out, and when the sandstone gets eroded, the quartz remains.

Q. At Clingmans Dome parking lot, what are the big gray boulders near the start of the walkway with the warning sign about the dangers of climbing on them?
A. Thunderhead Sandstone, very resistant to erosion and usually rounded.

Q. What are the sunken circles on those boulders?
A. The Thunderhead Sandstone is a conglomerate (mixture), and those circles show where a pebble of some softer material once was. Go down Forney Ridge Trail just a little way to see more of those strange circles. Also, if you rub your hand over the rock surface, you'll feel harder minerals, some of them bluish quartz pebbles, sticking out. These rocks are all part of the Ocoee Supergroup, made from the ancient ocean bed, but the Thunderhead Sandstone here was mixed with other materials during uplift.

Q. Is there coal in the Smokies?
A. Maybe waaaay down, where even mountaintop removal can't reach it. The rocks that make up the Smokies are Precambrian, formed when sea creatures had soft bodies that didn't leave many fossils. Coal formed in the later Carboniferous Era. The Cumberland Mountains of Middle Tennessee and mountains in West Virginia and Kentucky formed in the Carboniferous Era, and they are full of coal and fossils.

Q. The rocks at Newfound Gap look different. What are they?
A. The shale-like rocks to the right of the parking lot as you go in are Anakeesta (from a Cherokee word meaning "place of bal-

Arch Rock on Alum Cave Bluffs Trail was caused by freeze-thaw erosion of Anakeesta.

sams"). This rock has cleavage planes and a high iron content. When exposed, the iron rusts, making the rocks reddish and also releasing acids. Anakeesta is jagged and fragile. Don't climb there. The huge rock slide seen from the Newfound Gap road at the Morton Overlook was caused by freeze-thaw cycle that caused erosion of Anakeesta. Charlies Bunion, the jagged Sawteeth, Arch Rock, and Chimney Tops are also good examples.

Q. Why is the Anakeesta rock on Charlies Bunion exposed?
A. Two events cleaned off that promontory on the Appalachian Trail east of Newfound Gap. In 1925, fires started on logged slopes in North Carolina. The fire spread to the mountains tops and burned the heath balds. In 1927 a cloudburst washed away the damaged and unprotected soil. Plants are regaining a foot hold...or root hold. There's a little more sand myrtle and rhododendron every year on Charlies Bunion. Climbing there can be dangerous because Anakeesta Rock is both slippery and crumbly—several hikers have died on the Bunion.

Q. Who gave it that name?
A. Horace Kephart, in honor of the foot problems of Charlie Connors, who helped Kephart and George Masa hike up to observe the damage after the cloudburst.

"The **Tennessee River** system begins on the worn magnificent crests of the southern Appalachians, among the earth's oldest mountains, and...shapes its valley into the form of a boomerang, bowing it to its sweep through seven states. Near Knoxville the streams still fresh from the mountains are linked and thence the master stream spreads the valley most richly southward, swims past Chattanooga and bends down into Alabama to roar like blown smoke through the floodgates of Wilson Dam to slide becalmed along the crop-cleansed fields of Shiloh, to march due north across the high diminished plains of Tennessee and through Kentucky spreading marshes through the valley's end, where finally, at the toes of Paducah, in one wide glassy golden swarm the water stoops forward and continuously dies into the Ohio."
—James Agee, 1933

From Inspiration Point on the same trail you can see eroded holes in Duck Hawk Ridge.

PLANTS

Q. How many kinds of trees live in the Smokies?
A. About 135, more species than in all of Europe, and more than in any other U.S. national park.

Q. Why so many?
A. The mountains provide many different kinds of habitat—wet to dry, low elevation to high, valley and ridgetop, north and south exposure, varied soils.

At the Carlos Campbell Overlook, four miles from Sugarlands Visitor Center, a map display identifies eight forest types of the Smokies, and you can look out across the valley and see them all. This same map appears in many biology and ecology textbooks as an example of how plant communities relate to environmental conditions.

Cove hardwoods, one of the Smokies forest types, is a remnant of a species-rich forest that covered the eastern U.S., Europe, and Asia before the Ice Ages. Visit the Cove Hardwood Nature Trail at

Chimneys Picnic Area for an introduction to the Smokies' famous tree, wildflower, and animal diversity.

Q. If you had a time machine at Newfound Gap and could transport yourself back 20,000 years, what kind of vegetation might you see?
A. Alpine tundra, growing on permafrost. Brrrr.

Q. What makes the Smokies smoky?
A. The trees! And abundant moisture, of course. As the trees draw up water, they release vapor and volatile oils called terpenes that refract sunlight. So even when it isn't foggy, the mountains have a nice blue haze. But more recently, part of that smokiness has been caused by air pollution—not so nice.

Q. Is there virgin forest in the Smokies?
A. Yes, but biologists prefer to call it old-growth forest. About one-third of the forest in the park has never been cut.

Q. What's special about old-growth forest?
A. Number one, the trees are big and old. Some hemlocks in the park may be over 500 years old. The dense tree canopy of old-growth forest creates shade with little undergrowth. Other old-growth qualities: a diversity of plant and animal species, a mixture of young and old trees, rotting logs, and many special habitats.

Close to 90% of the old-growth forest in the eastern U.S. is in the Smokies. The park has more **champion** (biggest, tallest, or oldest of their kind) **trees** than any other U.S. national park. Examples: Tulip trees, blackgums, and Eastern hemlocks that are more than 500 years old, red spruce and white oak over 400 years old. On the Boogerman Trail near Cataloochee there is a white pine which was the tallest tree in the eastern United States at 207 feet (63 m) until 1995, when it lost a bit of its top to Hurricane Opal.

Q. How can they tell how old a tree is without cutting it down?
A. Dendrochronologists (botanists who study tree rings) extract

---

Poison ivy flourishes in the Smokies, but only below 3000 feet, and mostly in disturbed areas or young forest.

a small core sample from the tree, smaller than a pencil, and count the rings.

Q. How many lumber companies harvested in the future park?
A. In the early 1900s, twenty lumber companies operated in the Smokies and would have cut all the old-growth forest if the park hadn't been established.

Q. Do trees die of old age?
A. Yes, they can just get too big, or they can get too old to resist diseases, or they can get to be the tallest and get hit by lightning. Many huge tulip poplars in the park have lost their top halves in storms.

Q. How do little trees ever get a chance?
A. Most don't. But when a tree falls in the forest, young trees definitely hear it and start competing for the light. You can see patches of these eager young trees in the opening in the tree canopy near a fallen giant; the young trees often have leaves twice the size as normal for their species to grab even more of that light. The bigger leaves also help to shade out competitors. Or little trees might get a start on nurse logs.

Q. What is a nurse log?
A. A fallen tree that rots long enough that seeds can sprout in the moss on soft, punky wood. You can see nurse logs in Albright Grove, Boogerman Trail, and other old-growth places.

Q. What happens when the nurse log rots completely away?
A. Some of the trees look like they are standing on stilts where the roots grew around the nurse log to get to the ground. And sometimes you'll see a straight line of trees where the nurse log was.

Nettles are equal-opportunity annoyers—they grow at all elevations—but not on the grassy balds.

Q. When will areas that were logged just before the park was established become mature forest?
A. Check back in about 200 years.

Q. What happened to the American chestnut?
A. An Asian fungus blight, brought to this country on imported Chinese chestnut trees, killed almost all the chestnut trees in North America.

Q. How did it get around?
A. Tiny spores of the fungus spread very slowly from the New York Botanical Garden, probably traveling on birds' feet and feathers or the wind. It took the blight fungus 20 to 30 years to reach the Southern Appalachians.

Q. And how does this fungus kill big trees?
A. The fungus spores land in bark cracks and start growing thin threads into the live cells that live just under tree bark. The fungal threads kill these cells, so the leaves cannot get water and minerals and the roots cannot get sugars that the leaves make.

Q. So the American chestnuts are extinct?
A. No, when some of the trees died their roots stayed alive, and they keep sending up hopeful shoots that grow for a few years, but as soon as their bark starts to split, the fungus can get in and kill them.

Q. The blight is still around?
A. Yes, you probably just breathed in a few spores. It survives on oaks and other nut-bearing trees.

Q. Can anything be done to restore the chestnuts?
A. Researchers are developing resistant strains of American chestnut, either by crossing it with disease-resistant species such as

Southern magnolia, an evergreen, does not grow in the Smokies. But three close relatives—umbrella, Fraser, and cucumber magnolia—do, and they are deciduous (they drop their leaves in fall).

Chinese chestnut or finding a natural immunity in pure American chestnuts. They grow resistant chestnut trees in orchards and have planted thousands on abandoned strip mines. In 2008 and 2009, foresters planted many resistant chestnuts in undisclosed locations in the Smokies and the Cherokee National Forest, and they will study their survival.

Another approach is to infect American chestnuts with a hypo-virulent strain of the fungus to make them resistant to the real fungus when it floats in. Sound familiar? That's somewhat like vaccinating people with a cowpox virus (mild disease) to resist infection from smallpox (deadly disease).

Three reasons why the **American chestnut** was so important to the environment of the Smokies:
• They were the most numerous species—an estimated 30-40% of the trees in some areas were chestnuts.
• They were the biggest trees.
• They bloomed in May, after the danger of frost was past. Because of that, the chestnut crop was reliable food for wild-life every year, even when a late frost destroyed or reduced flowers of beeches, oaks, and hickories.

Three reasons why American chestnuts were valuable to settlers:
• The wood was rot-resistant.
• The trees were so big that the wood from one tree could build a whole cabin.
• People could gather chestnuts in fall and sell them—for some farmers this was their main cash crop.

And one more: People fattened up the hogs in fall by turning them out to find chestnuts.

Q. How did turkeys and ruffed grouse, with their skinny necks, swallow chestnuts?
A. Whole.

Q. Why are there so many dead trees at Clingmans Dome?
A. The gray skeletons you see there were Fraser fir trees. About

---

"The Earth laughs in flowers."—Ralph Waldo Emerson

95% of the firs died from an infestation of the balsam woolly adelgid, an aphid-like insect that was first spotted in the park on Mount Sterling in 1962.

Q. Does that insect attack other trees?
A. No, it attacks only that species. But there is a hemlock woolly adelgid from Asia that entered that park around 2003, and it is killing hemlocks at all elevations. The devastation of the hemlocks is especially visible along the Newfound Gap Road near the Chimney Tops.

Adelgids are so tiny you'd need a magnifier to see them, but you can see the white woolly fibers they spin to protect themselves and their eggs on the undersides of infected hemlock twigs.

Adelgid egg sacs under hemlock needles.

Like aphids, adelgids reproduce by parthenogenesis—that is, a female can reproduce without the help of a male. She just makes clones of herself, all female, and they can make clones, too. So one female adelgid blown in on the wind or stuck on a bird's foot can infect a whole tree.

Their saliva is toxic—it destroys the transport cells in hemlock needles.

Q. What is it about Asian insects and plant diseases?
A. Interesting question! Want the ancient geomorphology answer or the modern geopolitical answer?

Uh oh...time to go.

No, wait, it's not so complicated as it sounds. 60 million years ago—the Tertiary period, after the Age of Dinosaurs—a vast, continuous forest spread across what is now Asia and North America. It was warm and nice and alligators lived in Michigan. That forest was rudely interrupted by the uplift of the Rockies, by droughts, and, in Europe, by the glaciers smacking up against the Pyrenees and Alps. Remnants of that great forest survive in Asia and in the

---

As trees die and their roots rot, the network of roots that protects the forest from wind becomes weaker, and healthy trees may be blown over.

southern U.S. But the trees here have no immunity to a disease or pest that developed in Asia after the two sections of forest got separated. In other words, the balsam woolly adelgid gives Asian firs something like a cold, but it kills the firs here. Same with the Asian chestnut blight fungus.

Whew! OK, I guess I'm ready for the other answer.

Globalization. In the last hundred years or so we have been importing and exporting and mixing everything up. Think about kudzu and Japanese honeysuckle and dandelions—no natural predators, so they take over. Same with the adelgids.

Q. Why not bring some natural predators from wherever the adelgids came from?

A. Pretty risky, since scientists don't know what a species will do in a new environment. But some biologists have brought tiny lady bug beetles that seem to eat only hemlock woolly adelgids. After raising the predatory lady bugs in incubators (and asking them a lot of tough questions) they have released them into parts of the Smokies and the national forest to see if it can help the hemlocks survive. Ask a park ranger what the most recent evidence shows.

Q. Can those beetles reproduce in the park?

A. There is evidence that the introduced beetles have reproduced, but foresters don't know yet if they can reproduce fast enough or move around enough to save hemlocks.

Q. What else can the park do to protect the trees?

A. Some hemlocks near roads can be sprayed with a soapy solution, a treatment that has to be repeated. In some areas, such as along the first mile of Alum Cave Bluffs Trail, trees get injections or soil treatments. Park biologists can only protect a few of the hemlocks, but they have tried to create a patchwork of healthy hemlocks across the park that will help to reseed areas where others have died.

Q. How long do the injections and soil treatments protect the trees?

A. No one knows yet. One of the chemicals used to treat hemlocks is also used to control fleas and ticks on pets.

In 2010 the park was recruiting volunteers to inventory ash trees and others that may be attacked by invasive insects in the future.

Some reasons why it is important to save the **hemlocks:**
• Loggers didn't find much use for them, so much of the precious old-growth forest is hemlock stands.
• Some birds, bats, and other animals nest or feed only in hemlocks. Other species rely on them for parts of their life cycles. Most of the woodthrushes in the Smokies nest in hemlocks. One kind of fungus lives only on hemlock, and one kind of beetle eats only that fungus.
• Hemlocks keep stream water cold and soil moist.
• Hemlocks are beautiful.

Q. Are there other tree diseases?
A. Unfortunately, yes. Dogwoods, American beeches, ashes, mountain ashes, butternuts, and elms are being attacked by invasive pests and pathogens.

Q. What Smokies tree blooms in winter?
A. Witch hazel.

Q. How do the flowers get pollinated?
A. Most trees are smarter than they look. Witch hazel chooses a warm spell or thaw to bloom, and a few sleepy bees or flies come out then too.

Q. What Smokies plant can tell you the temperature in the winter?
A. Rhododendron. Its leaves curl to conserve water when it gets cold, and the colder it is, the tighter the curl. At freezing, the leaves droop. At 20 degrees F they start to curl, and at 0 degrees F they curl up smaller than pencils.

Q. What is the difference between rhododendron and laurel?
A. Rhododendron and mountain laurel are large (more than 10 feet or 3 meters tall) broadleafed evergreen shrubs in the same botanical family—the heath family. Rhododendrons often grow along creek banks or moist hillsides, while mountain laurels usually thrive on dry ridges. Trails through rhododendron and mountain laurel patches feel like tunnels, with the tangled branches closing overhead.

Chlorophyll makes leaves green. In fall, plants withdraw the chlorophyll, you can see other pigments that were there all the time: anthocyanin (red), carotene (orange) and xanthophyll (yellow).

Rhodendron

Q. How do you tell them apart?
A. Rhododendron leaves are longer (4-10 inches, or 10-25 cm) and more leathery than mountain laurel leaves (which range from 2-4 inches or 5-10 cm long). Rhododendron flowers have five pink petals with avocado-green spots on the uppermost petal. Mountain laurel flowers would make a nice design for a peppermint-candy cupcake—round and pink with darker pink stripes. In winter, only rhododendrons leaves curl.

Laurel

Q. What are rhododendron and laurel "hells"?
A. Rhododendron and mountain laurel branches twist and tangle with each other and with greenbrier and other grabby plants to form what early settlers called laurel hells, which are almost impossible to travel through.

Q. What Smokies shrub was used to attract boys?
A. Sweet shrub, or Calycanthus. The mountain name for it was bubby bush, and young ladies dropped the flowers down the fronts of their dresses. The flowers emit a pleasant smell when warmed.

Q. What Smokies plant can trip a witch?
A. Witch hobble, a high elevation shrub with beautiful, heart-shaped leaves. The plant makes a general tangle, but what really gets the witch is when a branch touches the ground and grows new roots, creating a firmly anchored loop. It even trips well-meaning hikers.

Q. What Smokies plant announces the return of a circuit-riding minister?
A. Service berry, or "sarvis" in mountain dialect. Its white blooms that show up early in the spring remind folks that winter is nearly over, the minister will soon be back, and if you've promised to marry someone, you'd better be ready to make good on it.

Some color names assigned by the American Rhododendron Society:
Goldilocks, Tequila Sunrise, Gregory Blush, Candy Stripe, Cover Girl.

Q. What Smokies tree flowers make the best honey?
A. Sourwood.

Q. How do you tell the bees to go to that flower?
A. You don't really need to. It blooms in the hot part of July when not much else is blooming, so the bees pick up on it right away.

Q. Which Smokies tree has four leaf shapes: regular, left-handed mitten, right-handed mitten, and mitten for three fingers??
A. Sassafras. This tree was also used for a health tonic until European explorers found another North American plant that (at that time) they thought was an even better health tonic: tobacco.

Q. Most leaves have pointy ends, possibly to help water drip off and to keep the leaf from being damaged in high wind. Which Smokies tree has a notch on the end with two points beside the notch, sort of like a cat's face?
A. Tulip-tree, or tulip poplar, a member of the Magnolia family, with beautiful flowers that look like lime, orange, and lemon sherbet.

Q. What Smokies tree is used for dowsing (finding underground water with a forked stick)?
A. Witch hazel. Some utility companies have hired dowsers.

Q. Which Smokies trees have seeds that spin like helicopters?
A. Many trees do: maples, tulip-trees, ashes, pines. Anything to get the next generation out of the house.

Q. What Smokies plant inspires a festival each May?
A. Ramps—wild leeks with a peculiarly

A handful of ramps.

Tulip-tree trunks are so straight that they were useful as shafts for wheels or mills; sourwood tree trunks bend at slight angles as they grow and were useful for sled runners.

strong and lasting taste and smell. Ramp collecting is not allowed in the Smokies, but ramp fans pick them in the national forests and fry them, put them in sandwiches, make smoothies, whatever. The odor sticks with you for days.

Q. Which Smokies plants have sperm that swim?
A. Ferns and mosses.

Q. This park is famous for its balds. What is a bald?
A. A bald is a high elevation exposed area that has no trees, so from a distance it looks bald. There are grassy balds, such as Spence Field, and heath balds, such as Brushy Mountain.

Trail across a Smokies bald.

Q. What caused grassy balds to form?
A. That's a botanical mystery. During Cherokee and European occupation, people kept the grassy balds open by burning and grazing, but no one is sure how they formed in the first place. Trees are now invading grassy balds in the Smokies.

In Cherokee myth, a huge hornet monster called Ulagu swooped into villages and carried small children off to its lair on the mountain tops. The people appealed to the Great Spirit for help. The Great Spirit sent lightning bolts to kill the Ulagu, and, in the process, burned the trees off mountain tops and high ridges. Ulagu's many children, the yellowjackets, are living proof of the legend.

The park maintains two grassy balds—Andrews Bald and Gregorys Bald—by cutting back the encroaching trees. (They tried goats and cattle, which did a good job, but required too much attention from herders.) The other grassy balds in the park shrink every year as trees grow in from the edges.

There are about 80 grassy balds in the southern Appalachians. Some people called them "Devil's footsteps."

Q. What about heath balds?
A. They have very acidic soils, and members of the heath family (rhododendron, mountain laurel, blueberries, sand myrtle) can thrive in the acidic soil, while most tall trees can't. Soil studies show that some heath balds formed hundreds of years ago, possibly from lightning fires.

Q. Which is the highest grassy bald in the park?
A. Andrews Bald, at 5700 feet. It's only two miles from Clingmans Dome parking lot.

Q. What's special about it?
A. Wildflowers in late spring, flame azaleas and Catawba rhododendrons in bloom in June, delicious blueberries in September, and great views all the time.

Q. Where is Gregory Bald?
A. It's one of the mountains surrounding Cades Cave.

Q. What's special about it?
A. Multicolored native hybrid azaleas, from pure white to deep red. The white and yellow ones smell better than honeysuckle.

Q. Why so much variety?
A. A combination of the right elevation (4950 feet) for four deciduous azalea species, an open grassy area free from livestock grazing, an abundance of pollinators such as bees and butterflies.

Q. When do the azaleas bloom on Gregorys Bald?
A. June 13-24, or thereabouts.

Q. Where else can you find these varieties of hybrid azaleas?
A. Nowhere, though the North Carolina Botanical Garden is trying to replicate them with cuttings.

Q. What else blooms on Gregory Bald?
A. Mountain laurel and Catawba rhododendron. Blueberries and blackberries abound in August.

---

175 species of plants have been found on Gregory Bald.

Q. What's unusual about the blackberries that grow above 6000 feet?
A. They have no thorns, even though they are the same kind as thorny ones at lower elevation. Botanists speculate that deer, elk, and bison didn't go high in the mountains, and the blackberry plants stopped producing thorns. Plants are smarter than they look.

Q. Carrion flower is a high-elevation vine with a ball of white flowers about the size of a baseball. How does it get pollinated?
A. It smells like a nicely rotting dead animal and attracts flies as pollinators.

Q. Why are there so many spring flowers?
A. Small plants need sun, so they get a head start before the trees make leaves and shade the ground. After they flower, they make and store enough food for a fast start the next year. Each species has a different "fiscal year" (March 1st to February 29 or April 15 to April 14, for example), and each spring its flowers depend largely on the "budget" of the year before.

Q. The park is famous for its trilliums (25 different kinds). How can you recognize a trillium?
A. It has three (or three pairs) of everything—petals, sepals, leaves, stamens, and stigmas. Most are white, but there is one yellow species and some with burgundy petals.

Q. Are there orchids in the Smokies?
A. Yes, several kinds. Lady's slippers, rattlesnake plantain, twayblades, and others. Most orchids are semi-parasitic—they make some of their food by photosynthesis but suck the rest from the roots of other plants.

Q. It's against the law to remove wild plants from the Smokies (or any national park). If people poach orchids, the plants have

In 2009, rangers caught poachers stealing several hundred ginseng roots. The roots that were not damaged have been replanted, and the poachers face prosecution in federal court.

an especially hard time surviving the transplanting. Why?
A. Orchids (as well as many other plants) have a symbiotic relationship with a fungus called mycorrhiza. The mycorrhiza works as a go-between for the orchid and other plants that the orchids get food from. If a new place has no mycorrhizae or doesn't suit them, the orchid will die.

Q. What is the biggest flower in the Smokies?
A. The flower of the umbrella magnolia tree—as big around as a small-medium pizza. It also has the biggest leaves (up to 24 inches or 50 cm) and the biggest buds.

Q. Is ginseng common in the Smokies?
A. No, it's rare because of overharvesting. In 1787 Daniel Boone collected 15 tons of ginseng root to sell in the cities, and many other people have made a lot of money from this slow-growing plant. Ginseng digging is illegal in the park, but poachers still steal it for black markets in Asia.

Q. Where can we see ginseng?
A. Sorry, won't tell.

Q. What do the following flowering plants have in common? Dodder, Indian pipe, squaw root, and beech drops.
A. They do not make chlorophyll and cannot make their own food. So—surprise—they're not green. Dodder doesn't even have roots or leaves—it climbs up other plants and sucks food from their stems. They are all parasitic (get their food from a living host) or saprophytic (suck up dead organic material).

Q. Filmy angelica, a tall, summer-blooming flower, bribes bees and wasps to carry pollen from one flower to another and not waste any pollen on other flowers that might be blooming in the area. How does it do that?

Indian pipe and squaw root, parasitic plants with no chlorophyll, have tiny vestigial leaves that look like hangnails.

A. Drugs! The angelica produces drugs (note: these are poisonous to humans) that make the bees and wasps high. After they stagger off one angelica flower, they sleep it off somewhere and then need another fix. So guess which kind of flower they look for!

Q. How many species of ferns are in the Smokies?
A. 44.

Q. What is a lichen?
A. A lichen is the result of a symbiotic relationship between a fungus and an alga. The fungus provides a structure of threads, and the alga can photosynthesize and provide food. Here's how to remember: A fungus took a lichen to an alga, and the marriage is on the rocks.

Q. Lichens on rocks often have a rounded shape and never seem to bump into each other. Why not?
A. Chemical warfare! Lichens protect their territory with chemicals that kill or inhibit other species.

Q. How do lichens reproduce?
A. Mostly by fragmentation—bits of the lichen break off and, if they land on a suitable surface and nothing else is claiming it, they attach and start growing...and arming themselves with chemicals.

Q. How many lichen species live in the Smokies?
A. Around 600.

Q. Fungi aren't plants, but here they are in the plant chapter. In what ways are they different from plants?
A) They have cell walls.
B) They can't make their own food.
C) They don't need oxygen.

Lichens grow very slowly, so if you scrape some off a rock, you may be removing a few hundred years worth.

A. B. Fungi cannot make their own food and send out threads to get food from living or dead organisms. Biologists used to place fungi in the Plant Kingdom, but now they have a kingdom of their own in biology textbooks.

Q. How many fungi species are in the park?
A. 2,250 and counting. They really deserve their own chapter.

Q. The following items grow in the Smokies. Decide for each if it's a tree, shrub, wildflower, fern, moss, lichen, or fungus.
1) Hearts-a-bustin'-with-love
2) Rock tripe
3) Adder's tongue
4) Fly poison
5) Turkey tail
6) British soldiers
7) Maiden hair
8) Stinking willie
9) Bracken
10) Sweetgum
11) Pussy toes
12) Sang
13) Destroying angel
14) Sarvis
15) Quaker ladies
A. 1) Shrub with bright magenta seeds that pop out of an orange pod
2) Lichen; also called pot-scrapings
3) Fern with a reproductive frond that sticks up like a snake's tongue
4) Wildflower in the lily family
5) Fungus that grows on dead tree trunks and looks like a turkey tail with feathers spread
6) Lichen with a green stalk and bright red top
7) Fern that is fan-shaped and feels soft
8) Wildflower—a trillium that stinks
9) Fern that grows up to three feet tall (1 m) on dry ridges
10) Tree that grows mostly at low elevations
11) Wildflower that blooms early in spring

_____

Mosses also defend their territory with chemical warfare.

12) Wildflower—ginseng
13) Fungus—a deadly poisonous Amanita mushroom
14) Tree in the rose family
15) Wildflower also known as bluets, or innocence

Q. The park has been very involved in an ATBI program since 1998. What does ATBI stand for?
A) Annelids and Thyracines as Bioindicators of Infestations
B) Adaptive Training of Beneficial Insectivores
C) Animal-Tourist Behavioral Interventions
D) All Taxa Biodiversity Inventory
E) Appalachian Trail and Backcountry Improvements
A. D) All Taxa Biodiversity Inventory

Q. What does that mean?
A. It's research to catalog and learn about all forms of life (taxa) in the park. OK, they're scientists, and they insist on using odd words. But "taxa" is easier to write than "All plants, animals, fungi, protists, slime molds, bacteria, archaebacteria, and everything else that doesn't fit in any of those slots."

Q. What are slime molds?
A. Weird taxa, for sure. They aren't molds, so you can't lump them with fungi. They don't make their own food, so they're not plants. They can move, but they're not animals. They are slimy, but not all the time.

Q. What do they look like?
A. They can be bright colors—orange, red, yellow—or brown or white or...invisible without a microscope. One kind looks like yellow Cool Whip one day and like brown powder the next day.

Q. What do they eat?
A. Bacteria! Their food is everywhere, and they slime over surfaces like horror movie blobs to engulf their food.

The park was designated an International Biosphere Reserve in 1973 in recognition of the biological diversity, and a World Heritage Site in 1983 in recognition of cultural preservation.

Q. Are there a lot of kinds of slime mold?
A. Along with being the salamander capital of the world, the park is probably the slime mold capital with 124 species...and it might be the springtail capital as well.

Q. OK, back to ATBI. What about biodiversity?
A. The Great Smoky Mountains are a temperate rainforest with an amazing variety of habitats, and the park was established just in time to save some old-growth forest. So the diversity of life forms here reflect what was here before human settlement, a diversity that may rival that of tropical rainforests.

Q. Biologists have been coming to the Smokies for a long time. Don't they already know what's here?
A. They know the big stuff—bears, birds, trees, salamanders. But smaller life forms haven't been studied as much.

Q. Why is that important?
A. For one thing, the bigger taxa depend on the smaller ones...or get diseases from them. To understand an ecosystem, you have to know about all of its parts. The Smokies ATBI is recognized as the largest sustained natural history inventory in the world.

Q. How did the ATBI start in the Smokies?
A. A tropical ecologist, Dan Janzen, raised money and enthusiasm for a similar project in Costa Rican rainforests, saying that we are losing life forms faster than we can study them. The agency he worked with in Costa Rica used some of the money for other projects. A Smokies biologist, Keith Langdon, asked Janzen if he would consider a project in the Smokies. They invited taxonomists—scientists who study different taxa—to a meeting and 120 experts from different areas of biology showed up in Gatlinburg.

Q. How is ATBI funded?
A. Grants, donations, memberships. Most of the scientists volunteer their time, including the citizen scientists.

Q. Citizen scientists?
A. Retirees, interested people, hikers, amateurs, birdwatchers.

ATBI biologists have an annual meeting where they report their findings of the year, discuss educational possibilities, and have a Salamander Ball where they dress up as their favorite taxa.

For example, a group goes on fern forays several times a year, set up by a fern specialist. They have learned where each species of fern lives, what other taxa it associates with, and how the ferns change month-to-month and year-to-year.

Q. How can citizen scientists help with, say, flies—it's so hard to tell them apart?

A. Good example. There are collecting sites all over the park which volunteers check regularly. At the Appalachian Science Center at Purchase Knob, elementary school kids learn to separate flies from bees, spiders, and other creatures. (Hey, how did that earthworm get into the canopy collecting net?) High school students can be trained to separate them further. Then the narrower sample might be sent to a fly expert in, say, Arizona, who

ATBI participant on a Fern Foray.

can assign it to graduate students. All the information (GPS data, time, season, weather, species found) returns to ATBI data files, maintained by a non-profit organization called Discover Life in America (DLIA), which coordinates ATBI efforts.

Q. How many species of flies have been found in the park so far?

A. 165

Many other parks have followed the Smokies ATBI example and are performing their own inventories.

Q. What is the largest group of taxa found in the park?
A. Insects, with 20,000-30,000 species—no wonder they need experts to sort them out! This includes approximately 1,500 beetles, 1,000 moths, and 210 bees, but only 19 species of wasps.

ATBI Discoveries

A group of volunteers combed the downy soft hair of northern flying squirrels to see what species of blood-sucking lice and mites live there. They slipped the combs (those fine-toothed combs used to find head lice) into specimen bags and shook out any critters. Wait—aren't northern flying squirrels endangered? Yes—a wildlife officer had to be part of the group to actually capture the squirrels to assure their safety while contributing to louse science.
Squirrel hairs from the specimen bags were sent to a lab for DNA barcoding.

Other ATBI discoveries include:
• Velvet-leafed blueberry, a northern species.
• A giant earthworm (up to a foot long) that lives near the Appalachian Trail.
• Many waterbears—chubby little (OK, microscopic) predators that live on moss or tree bark. When the moss dries out, waterbears shrink into a cyst. When the good times return, waterbears pop out, sometimes after years.
• Many species of springtails. A researcher found one specimen of a springtail never before seen in the park...in fact, it hadn't been recorded since 1954 and that was in New York. Was it a true record? The researcher trained a group of fifth graders to collect and sort springtails, and the kids found several specimens of the "lost species."

Learn more (including how to identify what you see in the Smokies) at www.discoverlife.org *and* www.dlia.org/atbi.

"ATBI has enlisted experts on different kinds of organisms from all over....Assisted by volunteers and with only a shoe-string budget, they have built it into a major enterprise of biological research, as well as teaching center for students at every level from grammar school to PhD and postdoctoral programs."—E. O. Wilson, Harvard biologist

As of January, 2010, the ATBI has discovered and documented 907 species new to science and 6,589 species new to the park.

ATBI researchers have published more than 80 scientific articles about Smokies biology since the project started

ANIMALS

Q. How many grizzly bears live in the Smokies?
A. None.

Q. Did grizzly bears ever live in the Smoky Mountains?
A. No. Grizzlies came from Asia to Canada and the western U.S., but they never came east. Black bears evolved in North America and can be found in 41 of the 50 states.

Q. How many black bears live in the Smokies?
A. About 1,500—more now than at any time on record.

Q. How much does an adult black bear weigh?
A. Males average 250 lbs. (112 kg) and females average 100 lbs. (45 kg).

Q. When are bear cubs born?
A. While their moth-
er is asleep! (Well,
she may wake up to
make sure the new-
borns start nursing.)
Usually it's in Janu-
ary or February, and
the hairless, blind
cubs weigh less than a pound.

Q. How many cubs can a bear have?
A. One to five (two is normal) every other year. The cubs emerge
with their mother in March or April weighing about five pounds (2
kg) and covered with fur.

Mama bears protect their cubs, so never, ever approach a cub.
Their defense usually involves bluff charges, but don't count
on it. Also remember that in early spring Mama Bear has been
feeding her cubs for a couple of months without eating anything
herself—she is probably very hungry.

> Now you need to learn about **fecal plugs**. Imagine that you
> wanted to sleep for 3-4 months without having to get out
> of your warm bed for anything. Bears don't truly hiber-
> nate—they can wake up at times—but they want to keep the
> den clean. They form a fecal plug to avoid the need to go
> out and poop. In spring, of course, they need to unplug. It
> is said that squaw root, a plant that comes up in March, is a
> favorite bear laxative.

Q. Where do bears spend the winter?
A. Many black bears sleep in hollow trees trunks high above the
ground. A bear researcher at the University of Tennessee put radio
collars on bears to trace them in the winter and was surprised to
hear the radio signals coming from high up. So naturally he sent
his graduate students up the tree to investigate. (Remember, the
bear is just asleep, not in deep hibernation.)

Snakes cannot close their eyes.

Q. If they're not really hibernating, why do they spend winter in dens?
A. They can't find food in winter...if you can't eat, you might as well sleep.

Q. How fast can a black bear run?
A. Faster than you can—up to 30 mph (45 kph).

Q. So if you can't outrun a black bear, is it a good idea to play dead?
A. No! Black bears are scavengers and will often eat the remains of dead animals. So if you play dead convincingly, this is a bad strategy. It's better to back away slowly. If a bear charges, make noise and try to look bigger (wave arms, etc.). Smokies black bears usually retreat. If you see a bear cub, it's time for you to retreat; Mama Bear is not far away.

Q. Are black bears always black?
A. In the Smokies, yes, and in most of their eastern populations, they are black with a brown muzzle. In western states, the black bears (the same species) may be brownish, cinnamon, or even blond.

Q. What do black bears eat?
A. Berries, insects, nuts, carrion, salamanders, grubs. Sometimes black bears will prey on fawns or newborn elk calves.

> **Hiking hazard:** In late summer, ground-nesting yellow jacket nests are full of delicious grubs, and bears don't mind a few stings on the nose to get them. So you might come hiking along a trail after a bear has dug out a nest...and guess who the yellow jackets are going to blame it on? Watch for freshly dug earth on the side of the trail with a buzzing yellow cloud around it. Take a wide off-trail detour.

Q. How do bears get ready for winter?
A. Eat, eat, eat. A bear may gain up to 5 pounds (2 kg) per day in the fall if the mast (acorns, beechnuts, hickory nuts) crop is good.

Census data: At any moment in time, salamanders will outnumber all the other vertebrates in the park.

Q. How many people have been killed by black bears in the park?

A. One, on record, in May, 2000. The victim, a woman, was hiking alone, and no one witnessed the event. A young boy was attacked by a black bear in 2008, and his father chased the bear away. (The dad lost his shoes in the scuffle, and pieces of shoe were later found in the bear's stomach.) There have been only seven recorded injuries to humans in the past ten years, and they usually involve the bear attracted to human food. The park service has to kill any bear that harms a person; feeding bears does them no favors.

Q. Do black bears growl?

A. Mostly in the movies. Black bear cubs purr when nursing, and their mothers grunt in response. The cubs squeal when frightened; adult black bears huff and clack their teeth when frightened or angry.

Q. How well do they see and hear?

A. They see color and movement, but their distance vision may not be as good as ours (though it is hard to test). The hearing of black bears is probably about twice as good as that of humans, and their sense of smell...well, smell depends partly on how much nasal mucosa an animal has, and black bears have 100 times as much nasal mucosa as humans. Remember this when you're camping and craving a midnight snack in your sleeping bag.

Q. How does the park manage bears that get a taste for junk food?

A. Sometimes rangers trap a bear, tranquilize it, pull a tooth (the number of rings on the tooth indicates the bear's age), take a blood sample, and put on radio collars or ear tags. With luck, the bear will wake up with a terrible headache and toothache and an aversion to people and their food.

Q. What if the bear doesn't get the message?

Male snakes and some other male reptiles have two penises.

A. A last resort for repeat panhandlers or bears that might be dangerous is to relocate them or euthanize them. Rangers also post signs and close shelters and backcountry campsites with high bear activity. Bear management in the Smokies has improved as researchers learn more about them, and both bears and humans have a better time in the park because of it.

Q. If rangers relocate a bear, can it find its way home again? From how far?
A. Often they can. Bears moved within the park may be spotted back home in a month. One radio collared bear called Bear #75 provided some information on homing abilities in the 1980s. He discovered the delicious corn meal in the Cable Mill in Cades Cove and broke into the building. Rangers caught him in the act and moved him several times...he always came back to Cades Cove, and he didn't forget that corn meal. Finally they sent him to Jefferson National Forest in West Virginia. He was spotted in Harrison, Virginia, caught and released in Wytheville, arrested by police in Roanoke, and, sadly, finally shot in Johnson City, Tennessee.

Q. Are there wolves in the park?
A. There were gray wolves in the mountains until the 1890s. States paid bounties on them, and gray wolves disappeared from the eastern U.S. The National Park Service tried to reintroduce red wolves in Cades Cove and Tremont in the 1990s. The wolves had cubs, but the cubs did not survive, some because of parvovirus from wild dogs. Biologists recaptured the adults and returned them to wildlife refuges in North Carolina. There are no current plans to try again.

However, coyotes, moving in from northern states, have successfully introduced themselves, and they don't even have to wear radio collars or report in to government biologists.

Q. When were coyotes first seen in the Smokies?
A. 1982. They came from the west the long way—from Canada over to Maine and then down.

Queen snakes are picky. They eat only crayfish, and only when the crayfish are molting.

Q. What Smokies mammal has the most teeth?
A. The Virginia opossum, with 50. Sharp, too.

Q. How long is an opossum pregnancy?
A. 12.5 days. But then the babies live in the pouch for two months. After that they ride on Mom's back.

Q. How many babies do possums have and when?
A. Up to 15 in a litter; four to six is common. They are born in late winter. Some possums have a second litter in summer.

Q. Which Smokies mammal has the biggest teeth?
A. The European wild boar, introduced to North Carolina in the 1912 for hunting. The pigs escaped and now live in many parks and forests. They grow upper and lower tusks that may be as much as 8 inches (20 cm) long, and they sharpen the tusks by rubbing them together. You do not want to get close to a wild hog. They use their tusks for defense and for rooting in the soil for plant tubers, salamanders, and other food.

Q. Wild boar piglets are
    A) Mottled   B) Spotted   C) Striped
    D) Black like the parents   E) Pink
A. C) Striped.

Q. What is the only poisonous mammal in the park?
A. The short-tailed shrew. The poisonous saliva paralyzes insects or other prey, and the shrew can eat a leisurely fresh meal for several days because the prey doesn't die right away. Shrews need to eat about three times their body weight each day. The short-tailed shrew uses echolocation to find frogs, snakes, or salamanders that have the bad luck to be underground near them, and then use the poison to subdue the prey. The shrews do not hi-

Wild boars might have two litters of piglets a year.

bernate, so they may eat other animals that do. They don't use their poisonous saliva for self-defense, but they do produce nasty chemicals from skin glands. Sometimes foxes or weasels dig up shrews and kill them, but then get a whiff and don't eat them.

Q. How do bats catch prey in mid-air?
A. Two ways—the one you might expect, that is, grabbing flying moths by mouth. But they can also scoop large insects up in their wing and tail membranes and then reach down with their mouths to subdue and eat the prey...without falling out of the air.

Q. How do they do that in the dark?
A. Echolocation. The bat emits supersonic squeaks that bounce off objects such as prey or obstacles. Sound waves from the squeaks bounce back to the bat's big ears, and from the quality of the bounce-back, the bat can tell if it's a twig, another bat, or a delicious moth or mosquito. Some moths have counterstrategies—they can detect the squeaks and dive or even send back confusing sound waves.

Q. How many vampire bats live in the Smokies?
A. None reported so far; all 10 species of bats in the park are insectivores. They eat lots of mosquitoes, though, and may get some of your blood that way.

Q. Which bat in the Smokies is endangered?
A. The Indiana bat, which has a large hibernating colony in the White Oak Blowhole near Schoolhouse Gap. This cave is completely closed with heavy bars to protect the colony. If bats are disturbed during hibernation, they may use too much energy reacting to the threat and not make it through the winter, so even the most careful cavers may harm the bats.

Q. How long can Indiana bats live?
A. Up to 20 years. They mate in fall and give birth in June.

Q. What is the most common bat in the Smokies?
A. The eastern pipistrelle.

Female bats store sperm over the winter, so they can mate in August but not get pregnant until spring.

Q. The smallest?
A. The eastern small-footed bat, with a wingspan of 8.3 to 9.2 inches (21-25 cm). The largest is the hoary bat, with a wingspan of 14-16 inches (35-40 cm).

Q. How much do bats eat?
A. About half their body weight each night.

Q. What is a baby bat called?
A. A pup.

Q. What does a mother bat do with her pup while she's out hunting?
A. She hangs it up by its toes.

Q. How does she find her pup again in the dark?
A. Mother and pup recognize each other's squeaks.

Q. A bat's wings are stretched out like a section of an umbrella. What long bones serve as the spokes?
A. The bat's fingers.

Q. Do bats have thumbs?
A. They sure do. Bats' thumbs stick out from the wrist and can grab onto branches or cracks. Bats crawl with their thumbs.

Pipistrelle bats, besides having the prettiest name, have tricolored dorsal hairs—that is, each single hair has three colors—reddish on the tip, yellowish in the middle, and dark brown near the roots, and not just when the bat needs to go the beauty parlor.

The big brown bat has a 12-inch (30 cm) wingspan. It can live more than 10 years.

Q. What kinds of rabbits live in the Smokies?

A. Two species—the eastern cottontail at all elevations and mostly in open areas, and the Appalachian cottontail, at high elevations. It is nocturnal and rare.

> **Rabbits** produce two kinds of fecal pellets—green and brown. Huh? So what?
>
> Well, here's the deal. You're a tasty rabbit, so when you're out in the open, eating juicy clover, you gulp it down as fast as you can, before a hawk or great big snake sees you. Then you hop back to a safe briar patch or den and poop out the half digested pellets—still green. Then you go back for more. Later, yum...you eat the green pellets again and finish the digestion, and then poop out some brown pellets. You know about re-gifting; now you know about re-eating.

Q. What kinds of skunks live in the Smokies?

A. Two species—striped (common) and spotted (rare).

Q. What is the main predator of skunks?

A. Great horned owls. What does that tell you about an owl's sense of smell? Striped skunks rarely climb, so if you smell skunk up in a tree, look for an owl.

Q. What other owls live in the Smokies?

A. Screech owls, barred owls, and saw-whet owls, named for their call which sounds like a saw is being sharpened. Biologists tried to reintroduce barn owls into Cades Cove by hacking them—that is, raising them in a place to make them feel that it is home. The barn owlets grew up and flew away and haven't been seen since.

Q. Which of the following is true of owls:
A) They can turn their heads 360 degrees.

Bats rarely have rabies. But don't touch one anyway.

B) They cannot move their eyes in the sockets.
C) They cannot see in the daytime.
A. B) Their eyes are so big that they have to move their heads to look around.

Q. What is the largest kind of woodpecker in the Smokies?
A. The pileated woodpecker, sometimes called the Lord God bird because of what someone might say when seeing one suddenly. They are as big as chickens, with startling red crests. They have an amazing cackling laugh-like call.

Q. What is the smallest woodpecker?
A. The downy woodpecker, a modest little guy that runs up and down tree trunks and makes friendly chirps.

Q. How many mammal species live in the Smokies?
A. 65.

Q. All mammals are warm-blooded, right?
A. When they're active, yes. But when they hibernate, their body temperature might be just a few degrees above freezing.

Q. What rodent is most commonly seen in Cades Cove?
A. The woodchuck, also called whistle pig because it stands up and whistles when alarmed. Woodchucks are common in Cades Cove and along any park road.

Q. What's the difference between a woodchuck and a groundhog?

A. Where you grew up—these are regional names.

Q. Why are there fewer woodchucks in the park than there were in 1934?
A. Woodchucks prefer open grassy areas, like farm fields and pastures. After the park was created and settlers left, there were fewer fields. Woodchucks love the park management plan that calls for roadside mowing.

Acid rain makes it hard for snails to get calcium for their shells. Nesting birds depend on snails for calcium for their eggshells.

Q. What is the park's biggest rodent?
A. The beaver. It was hunted out, but has become reestablished in Abrams Creek and some other places. Some beavers dig burrows in creek banks instead of building dams. The beavers in the park probably came from reintroduction projects in parts of North Carolina.

Q. How big is a beaver?
A. Up to 65 lbs. (30 kg)

Q. Where are a beaver's lips?
A. Behind its teeth—great for gnawing underwater and carrying branches without getting a mouthful.

Q. Which is the smallest Smokies mammal?
A. The pygmy shrew, weighing less than a penny. Don't spend much time looking for one—they live underground.

Q. What sorts of other small rodents live in the park?
A. Four species of voles, one lemming, two kinds of jumping mice, the Allegheny woodrat, and the golden mouse, which spends a lot of time high up in trees. The one you're most likely to see (and hear) is the eastern chipmunk.

Chipmunks build elaborate dens up to three feet below ground. They collect nuts and grains all summer long, carrying the food back in their cheek pouches to fill many pantries in the dens. In fall, they go into high gear, collecting more and more, and when one chipmunk is out, another may raid its pantries.

Q. Bears make fecal plugs so the den stays clean all winter. How do chipmunks solve that problem?
A. One room in the den (probably the last door on the right) is the bathroom.

Q. What about squirrels?
A. Gray squirrels, fox squirrels, and red squirrels live in the Smokies. If you do any hiking at high elevation, you'll meet the red squirrels, or boomers.

"A world of mountains piled upon mountains."—William Bartram, 1791, describing his first views of the southern Appalachians

Q. Why are they called boomers?
A. Because they have so much to say. They have strong opinions, and they don't mind telling you about them. Other mountain names for them are chickaree and fairy diddle.

Red squirrels store food in middens; they also have special perches on stumps or rocks where they gather food and stand there to eat it. With eyes on the sides of their heads, they can see front and back to watch for predators. If you see a stump covered with nutshells, listen for the squirrel hollering at you to move along.

Two species of **flying squirrels** live in the park—the southern flying squirrel and the endangered Carolina northern flying squirrel. These rodents aren't squirrels and they don't fly—they glide using flaps of skin stretched from arms to legs. They eat lichens and fungi as well as berries, nuts, and an occasional bird egg.

Q. Why do some rodents have red teeth?
A. Their tooth enamel is reinforced with iron compounds, the better to gnaw with.

Q. Which mouse is the most common in the Appalachian Trail shelters?
A. Deer mouse. They love to run up sleeping bags and jump on noses.

Before the park was established, hunting and trapping wiped out the **river otters**. Starting in 1986, otters captured in South Carolina and Louisiana were released on Abrams Creek and then other major creeks. The otter reintroduction project did well, and today otters breed in the park and in surrounding areas.

One Appalachian Trail thru-hiker took a cat along. The cat rode on top of the hiker's pack and caught shelter mice at night. The cat gained a lot of weight between Georgia and Maine.

Q. What do otters eat?
A. Slow-moving fish and salamanders, but their favorite food is crayfish.

Crayfish on a creek bottom.

Raccoons and otters search underwater for **crayfish**. After a "lobster" feast, they poop out shell bits and stomatoliths. What are stomatoliths? *Stomato* = stomach and *lith* = rock. Crayfish shells require calcium. When the crayfish molts, it absorbs the shell calcium and stores it in the stomach as a hard, white stone, so that the calcium can be recycled into the new shell.

Q. Do mountain lions live in the Smokies?
A. It depends on who you talk to. The 2009 *Mammals of the Smokies* book lists them as "extirpated." Early settlers and loggers did the "extirpating." Bobcats, however, are doing just fine, as are red foxes.

Q. How big are bobcats?
A. About 11-30 lbs (5-14 kg), approximately twice as big as a

domestic cat. They have longer legs, bigger ears, and bigger toe pads than domestic cats.

Q. How can you recognize bobcat tracks?
A. Bobcats, like domestic cats, retract their claws while walking. This keeps the claws clean and sharp and also improves stealth. Tracks of other Smokies carnivores show claw marks.

Q. What's the difference between a bobcat and a lynx?
A. Lynxes are larger, live in northern habitats, and have larger ear tufts than bobcats. The two are closely related, though (in the same

There are 700 miles (1,120 km) of fishing streams in the Smokies. Tennessee or North Carolina fishing licenses are valid in the park.

genus), and breeders have crossbred lynx and bobcat for their fur.

> **Bobcats** range across the United States and into Mexico, with different subspecies adapted to deserts, swamps, and mountains. They all have round pupils, not the football-shaped pupils of domestic cats.

Q. What is the range of red foxes?
A. Across the entire northern hemisphere—Alaska to Tibet and China. With a little help from their friends in red hunting coats, red foxes were brought to the southern United States in the 1600s and spread across the continent faster than European human settlers did.

Q. What color is the tip of a red fox's tail?
A. Always white. The slightly larger gray fox has a black-tipped tail.

Q. Are red foxes more like cats or dogs?
A. Biologically, they are canids, or members of the dog family. But they resemble domestic cats in size, manner of stalking prey, and in having vertical slit pupils.

Q. How many species of snakes live in the park?
A. 21.

Q. Which ones are venomous?
A. Only two: copperhead and timber rattler.

Q. How many people die each year of snake bite in the park?
A. None. And there is no recorded human death from a copperhead bite.

Q. How many snake bites are recorded?
A. Up to three a year; most years none are reported.

Copperhead

Foxes eat berries, apples, grapes, and other fruit. Their main diet may include more invertebrate prey (grasshoppers, worms, etc.) than vertebrate.

Q. How many snakes die from interactions with humans?
A. Unknown, but snakes are protected along with all other park species. This was not always the case—early park managers and rangers thought snakes should be killed, venomous or not. And before the park? We're lucky to have any snakes at all; their secretive habits saved them from the fate of other predators.

Q. What snakes are most commonly seen along the trails?
A. Probably garter snakes—skinny brown or gray with yellow or pale stripes along the body. Another commonly seen snake is the black rat snake. It can climb right up the trunk of a tree. Both of these snakes may freeze when hikers approach to help their camouflage. The black rat snake may stiffen its body to look more like a stick. And if that doesn't work, it might rattle its tail against dry leaves. Many non-venomous snakes imitate rattlesnakes this way. It can be pretty convincing!

Q. Can all snakes bite?
A. Yes, but they do only if they're cornered or grabbed. Wouldn't you?

Any **snake** that is
- All green OR
- Skinny OR
- Solid color with no pattern OR
- Striped from head to tail

Belongs to one of the non-venomous species.

Q. Snakes lay eggs, right?
A. Well, partly right. Constricting snakes (rat snakes, corn snakes) lay eggs in a protected place and then leave. But garter snakes, water snakes, copperheads, and rattlesnakes give birth to live young, usually in August. They don't do much parental care either, though some rattlesnake families will cuddle together a few days after the blessed event.

Q. Are there any vegetarian snakes?
A. No, they all eat some kind of meat—slug meat, bug meat, mouse meat, or fish.

Copperheads shake their rattle-free tails when disturbed, causing a "rattle" sound from dead leaves they are touching.

Q. Where do snakes hibernate?
A. For most snakes it's a secret. However, rattlesnakes and copperheads and sometimes other non-venomous snakes have communal dens on south-facing rocky places (which get warm first in spring). This is handy, because the first item on the agenda in spring is mating. Then the snakes disperse and may not see each other again until fall.

Q. What is the largest animal in the park?
A. Elk, which are the largest members of the deer family, used to be common in the east but were hunted out more than a century ago.

Q. So how big are they?
A. 250-800 lbs.g (110-360 kg); up to five feet (150 cm) at the shoulder.

Q. When were elk reintroduced into the park?
A. In 2001, 25 elk were released in Cataloochee, and in 2002, 27 more were released. All of the elk wear radio collars; elk calves are captured and given a collar a few months after birth.

Q. How are they doing?
A. Quite well, thank you. In 2009, 19 elk calves were born, and 16 survived. Bears will prey on newborn calves and some may have been lost that way. The population in the park was 110 in 2009. One of the original adults, #21, died in 2009.

Q. What happened to Elk #21?
A. On November 12, 2009, a poacher shot #21 inside the park boundaries. The poacher was caught and will be prosecuted. Friend of the Smokies set up a Memorial Fund for #21—the funds will be used to continue monitoring the elk program.

Q. How do the bears find newborns elk after their mothers have hidden them?
A. It just happens that elk calving time is about when the wild strawberries get ripe on the meadows of Cataloochee. At first, bears stumbled on elk calves while nosing around for strawberries, but they learned very quickly to search

---

You can often see elk near the Oconaluftee Visitor Center. One time an elk startled a horse at the Mountain Farm Museum, and they both galloped up the Blue Ridge Parkway.

the whole area. Rangers learn quickly, too; for a few years, rangers captured the bears that hang out near Cataloochee and moved them to another part of the park. By the time the bears got home, the elk calves could take care of themselves. No bears were moved in 2009, and it turns out elk mothers learned a little something, too—they now hide their calves away from the open parts of the meadow.

Q. At what age do male elk have their largest antlers?
A. Around 10 years old. Like all deer, elk shed the antlers every year and grew new and bigger ones for the next rut, or mating season. The elk rut in Cataloochee in September is quite a tourist attraction; the elk are not shy.

Q. How much can a pair of elk antlers weigh?
A. Up to 40 lbs (18 k).

Q. Who supplied funds for the elk reintroduction?
A. The Friends of the Smokies, the Great Smoky Mountains Association, and the Rocky Mountain Elk Foundation.

Q. True or false: Elkmont was named for the elk herds found there when settlers arrived.
A. False. Elkmont was established as a vacation community by the Benevolent and Protective Order of Elks (BPOE) of Knoxville.

Q. How many upper incisors (cutting teeth) do deer and elk have?
  A) None   B) 4   C) 6
A. A) none.

Q. How many species of deer live in the Smokies?
A. Only one, the white-tailed deer.

Q. How many white-tailed deer live in the Smokies?

Deer have four stomachs. While exposed to danger in a meadow, they eat and swallow quickly. Later, in a safer place, they regurgitate the food and chew it again.

A. Probably more than 6,000. That's up from an estimated 30 from when the park was formed in 1934.

Q. Why so few deer in 1934 and so many now?
A. By 1934, overhunting, aided by logging roads and railroads, almost wiped out the deer population. But since then, park protection, absence of wolves and cougars, and introduction of deer in other areas of the South have allowed deer populations to increase dramatically.

Q. Do whitetail does usually have single or twin fawns?
A. They usually have single fawns between May and August, but in good years they may have twins or triplets.

Q. Where is the best place in the park to see deer?
A. Cades Cove and Cataloochee. But often, when you're hiking in the woods, you can glance up a slope and see deer watching you go by.

Q. How big are the park's whitetail deer?
A. They weigh 75-250 lbs (35-113 kg). A newborn fawn weighs about 6 lbs (2.7 kg).

Q. When is the mating season for deer?
A. October through December.

Q. Deer and elk lose their antlers in early spring. Why don't we see antlers lying around?
A. Antlers contain calcium, a very valuable commodity in forest ecosystems. As soon as they hit the ground, something will eat them—mice, voles, or snails. And, as soon as the mice turn the calcium into their own bones, an owl is going to want that calcium for her egg shells...and so on. After bird nesting season, you don't see many eggshells lying around, either.

Q. How many species of trout live in the Smokies?
A. Three—native brook trout and introduced brown trout and rainbow trout.
    Decades ago, non-native trout were stocked in the creeks, and

---

Male fawns grow a single pair of spike antlers in their first fall. In later years, they grow branched antlers with more points each year as long as they are strong and healthy.

they out-competed the native brook trout. Now, however, the brook trout have been restored to several stream systems, and the forests that are recovering from the logging era now protect the streams and keep them cool and clear enough for brook trout.

The Smoky Mountain brook trout, sometimes called spec because of its speckles, used to be so common that a boy could catch a hundred or so in an afternoon in Cataloochee, and there are similar stories from other parts of the park. Then, with environmental damage from logging and competition from the introduced trout, the park feared that the spec might be in danger. In the last three decades, trout management (removing nonnative trout from watersheds, controlling fishing) seems to be improving the native trout population.

Q. Can you fish for trout in the park?

A. Yes. You can fish for brook trout year-round—with two exceptions: Bear Creek at its junction with Forney Creek in North Carolina, and Lynn Camp Prong above its confluence with Thunderhead Prong in Tennessee. You must have a valid fishing license from either of these states.

Q. What is stickbait?

A. Caddisfly larva. These larva make houses out of sticks and web (or other materials) and glue the houses (or maybe we should call them sleeping bags) to rocks in fast-moving streams. The larva reaches out from the stick structure and captures small prey that swim or float by. (Some caddisfly larvae construct a tiny seine net.) Then it retreats into the stick bag where predators can't get at it. However, kids wanting to fish for trout can easily find the larva, tear it out, and use it for bait on a small hook. Use of stickbait, worms, or any other live bait is not allowed in the Smokies today. But you can find caddisfly larva in almost any Smokies creek by gently turning rocks. Put them back carefully.

Q. What else might be on creek stones?

A. Mayfly larvae, stonefly larvae, egg masses, water mites, hel-

---

The peregrine falcon is the fastest flier in the park and often stuns prey by slamming into it in midair.

gramites, dragonfly larvae. All of the larvae living on creek stones are amphibious. At the end of their larval stage, they will crawl up a rock or plant stem, split their skin right down the back, and emerge as winged insects. You can often find the empty skins.

Four species of **native non-game fish**—the Smoky Mountain madtom, the yellowfin madtom, the spotfin chub, and the duskytail darter apparently died out from Abrams Creek. Researchers found populations of these endangered fish in Citico Creek in the Cherokee National Forest. They collected eggs and released hatchlings in Abrams Creek, and the reintroduction has succeeded.

Q. How many species of birds live in the park?
A. About 240 species have been reported. Most are neotropical migrants—that is, they spend winter in South or Central America and come to the Smokies to breed.

Q. Do all Smokies birds migrate?
A. No, many stay in the park all year long. Some migrate vertically—they nest at high elevation, but fly down the mountain to warmer valleys in winter. One bird, the dark-headed junco, is called the snow bird because folks who live in the valleys only see it in winter.

Peregrine falcons were last reported in the park in 1942. They were victims of DDT poisoning and couldn't incubate their eggs because the shells became too soft to sit on. In 1984-86, park biologists reintroduced 13 peregrine falcons to Greenbrier Pinnacle. In 1997, a pair of peregrines raised three chicks on Little Duck Hawk Mountain, near Alum Cave. Duck Hawk is another name for Peregrines...now how did those introduced falcons know which was their mountain?

Some migratory birds, such as the white-throated sparrow, stop to enjoy spring in the Smokies for a few weeks and then fly on to New England, where they nest.

Q. What does "peregrine" mean?
A. It means "wandering." The same species of peregrine falcon lives all across the United States and in Europe, and in all areas they almost became extinct, and because of many reintroduction programs, the species is recovering.

Q. If it's a wandering falcon, how did the park biologists persuade the reintroduced birds to stay here?
A. Falcons (and many other birds) feel "at home" only in a place where they grow up. So biologists have to reintroduce nestlings, and they face two problems: How to raise the chicks as well as a bird parent could, and how to keep the birds from getting used to people. They raised peregrine falcons on a tower on a mountain near Greenbrier that was temporarily closed to hikers, and they cared for the chicks feeding them with hand puppets.

Q. How fast do peregrines fly?
A. Pretty fast in general, but when they dive, they clock in as the world's fastest flier—about 180-200 mph (290-320 kph). They prey mostly on birds and dive at them, stun or kill them with a blow with the talons, and then swoop beneath the prey to catch it before it falls to the ground.

Q. What Smokies bird has the longest song?
A. The winter wren, one of the park's smallest birds. Its song can last for up to 10 seconds, with a variety of trills and warbles. Loud, too. Winter wrens often sing all day and sometimes answer each other, one starting to sing as soon as the first quits.

Q. How big is the winter wren?
A. About 4 inches (10 cm), a bit smaller than the more common Carolina wren.

Q. What is the park's smallest bird?
A. Ruby-throated hummingbird, the only hummingbird species in the eastern U.S. An adult is less than 4 inches (10 cm) long, and its heart can beat 600 times a minute.

Turkeys just barely survived the overhunting and habitat destruction of the early 20th century, but their population increased slowly until the 1960s, and now they are quite common.

Q. What are owl pellets?
A. Neat packages of tiny rodent or bird bones wrapped in fur. When an owl or hawk eats an animal, it separates the meats and guts from the indigestible parts and regurgitates the package. Biologists can collect the pellets to study what birds of prey are eating without bothering the birds.

Q. Which bird has feathers growing on its beak?
A. The common raven.

Q. What's the difference between a raven and a crow?
A. Ravens, at a length of 24 inches (60 cm) are about $^1/_3$ larger than crows. Their bills are longer and thicker. Crows may be found at all elevations of the park, while ravens usually stay at the higher elevations and cliff tops. Ravens often soar on thermals and do aerial acrobatics.

> Bad joke: How do you tell a raven from a crow? Well, the raven has one more large wing feather on each wing, so it's really just a matter of a pinion.

Q. You see a large black bird hopping around the Sugarlands or Oconaluftee visitor center parking lot. What is it?
A. It's probably an American crow.

Crows

Q. You see a large black bird hopping or walking around the Clingmans Dome parking lot. What is it?
A. It's almost certainly a common raven.

Raven

Q. Which bird has feathers on its toes that work like snowshoes?
A. The ruffed grouse.

Vulture chicks defend themselves by projectile vomiting. And when you consider what their parents have been feeding them...

Q. Most birds are naked and helpless when they hatch, and the parents feed them, keep them warm, and clean up after them until they fledge. What Smokies birds walk and feed themselves from day 1 after hatching?
A. Ruffed grouse and turkey.

Q. How many eggs do hen turkeys lay?
A. Ten to twelve, in a feather-lined nest on the ground. Like domestic chickens, they lay one egg a day until the clutch is complete, and then they incubate for 28 days. The chicks, or poults, become imprinted on their mother's call and follow her away from the nest right after hatching.

Q. How can we see a salamander?
A. Walk in the rain! Or look in the splash zones of waterfalls. A flashlight helps.

The southern Appalachians, especially the Smokies, are called the **salamander capital** of the world. There are more than 30 species in the park, and they are ecologically impor-tant as predators of insects and other small invertebrates. Many have no lungs—they get all of their oxygen through their moist skin. For this reason, it is not good to handle salamanders—would you want someone grabbing you by your mucous membranes?

Q. What is the largest salaman-der in the Smokies?
A. Hellbenders. Also known as snot otters for their gobs and gobs of skin slime.

Salamander

Q. How big are hellbenders?
A. 12-30 inches long (30-75 cm); a big one can be longer than some cats.

Q. What is the main predator of hellbender eggs?
A. Other hellbenders. A male hellbender chooses a nest and per-suades as many females as he can to come in and lay eggs. Then

---

The red-cheeked salamander (all black except for the bright red cheeks) lives only in the Smokies and can be found at middle to high elevations.

he fertilizes them and protects them from other hellbenders until the larvae hatch and swim away.

Q. Where do hellbenders live?
A. In the lower parts of Little River, Deep Creek, and Oconaluftee River. They depend on clear, clean, running water.

Q. What is the difference between a lizard and a salamander?
A. Lizards are reptiles (so they are related to snakes and turtles), while salamanders are amphibians (related to frogs and toads). Lizards have scales, live mostly on land (and inhabit the driest parts of the park); salamanders have soft, wet skin and must stay in or near water to get oxygen and reproduce. If you see a salamander, its body form might look lizardy, but check its pop-up eyes, which definitely look froggy.

Q. How many species of lizards are there in the park?
A. Nine, but the two most common are the fence lizard and the five-lined skink. The glass lizard is legless—it looks like a snake, but it has two things a snake lacks: ears and a tail that will break off to confuse or distract predators. Glass lizards are rare in the Smokies.

Q. What is a newt?
A. A newt is a kind of salamander that has three life stages—larva, red eft, and adult (in other words, it has metamorphosis twice...imagine being a teenager twice). Newts are not common in the Smokies because there are so few ponds, but they might be seen around Cades Cove or near Gatlinburg.

Q. How many species of turtles live in the park?
A. Eight species. One, the Eastern spiny softshell, looks like a walking pancake. If you're hiking at mid-to low-elevation you might see a box turtle, the only land turtle in the park.

Q. What Smokies insects cause the park to close some roads and provide trolley services in June?
A. Fireflies! Synchronous fireflies.

Blue-tailed skinks (lizards) guard their eggs until the babies hatch. If the eggs start to dry out, the mother pees on them.

Q. They all flash together?
A. Yes, they put on a wonderful light show.

Q. Where and when?
A. In Elkmont, along the road that goes by the old summer cabins, Between June 5 and 25, depending on the weather.

Q. How can we see them?
A. Trolleys take visitors from Sugarlands parking lot at dusk. People bring chairs and picnics and settle in for a few hours.

Q. Why do the fireflies flash in synchrony?
A. Male fireflies flash to impress females. They fly around a few feet above the ground and flash together for several seconds and then all stop for an interval of complete darkness. Sometimes it's like a wave in a sports arena. Why synchronous? Only the fireflies know for sure. Among 14 species of fireflies in the park, only one, Photinus carolina, flashes synchronously.

Q. What do the females do?
A. They crawl in the grass and respond with flirty flashes so the males can find them.

For many years, a scientist at Georgia Southern University traveled to remote parts of Asia to study **synchronous fireflies.** Someone who had a cabin in the Smokies saw a research report and contacted the professor to say that she had synchronous fireflies on her lawn every June; now he drives up to Tennessee for his research.

Q. What's the difference between a firefly and a lightning bug?
A. Where you grew up.

Sometimes a female firefly of another species crashes the party. She flashes to a handsome male, and when he comes down to mate with her, she eats him. Talk about a bad date.

Fence lizards, on the other hand, just drop their eggs in a hole and cover them with dirt.

Animal signs quiz—match the animals under Q. with the marks they leave, listed under A.

Q. 1) Horizontal rows of pencil-point-sized holes on a tree trunk, as if someone had drilled them in a straight line with a power drill.

2) An oblong hole in a dead tree about the size of a dollar bill.

3) The remains of a spruce cone with all the scales chewed off except a little tuft at the end.

4) Many holes along the side of the Appalachian Trail, looking like just the right size for bees or yellow jackets.

5) Redbud or magnolia leaves with C-shaped cutouts along the edges.

6) Large trailside areas that look plowed or rototilled.

7) A papery brown hollow sphere like a rough table tennis ball, sometimes attached to a piece of an oak leaf.

8) A chimney made of mud beside a creek with the opening about the size of a man's thumb.

A. 1) Yellow-bellied sapsucker. This small woodpecker drills the holes and then comes back to drink the sap and to eat any insects that have gotten trapped in the sticky fluid.

2) Pileated woodpecker. Sometimes you can see scraps of wood that the woodpecker tossed over its shoulder.

3) Red squirrel, or boomer. They also drop magnolia or tulip-tree flowers on the trail.

4) Appalachian Trail backpackers, using their hiking poles.

5) Leaf-cutter wasps. They cut out these neat shapes, carry them to a tree trunk, roll them up like tiny cigars, lay their eggs in them, and then push them out of sight in a bark crevice.

6) Invasive wild boars.

7) A gall wasp. The wasp stings an oak leaf and lays her eggs on it. The leaf grows the gall around the eggs in response to the irritation. When the eggs hatch, they eat the oak tissue, drill a little hole, and fly off. The empty husk falls on the ground.

8) Crayfish. They burrow away from the creek and build the chimney so they can get air but be protected from raccoons, otters and other predators.

"If you approach an animal so closely that it stops feeding, changes direction of travel, or otherwise alters its behavior, you are too close."—Park brochure

Q. Are there other park nature shows like that?
A. Male elk bugle in September and October in Cataloochee. Hundred of park visitors gather to watch the rut, which includes loud bugling, sparring, and rubbing antlers on trees. Same reason—to impress the females.

Q. Does the park have other seasonal spectacles?
A. In April, thousands of people come to the Wildflower Pilgrimage in Gatlinburg. This one's about sex, too—flower sex. Spring flowers display to attract pollinators to take the pollen from one flower to another.

> About 100 species of **snails** live in the park—from pinhead size to the golf-ball-sized pulmonate (with one lung) land snails that you can see out and about in rainy, misty, or even humid weather.

Q. Which are more numerous—moths or butterflies?
A. There are many more species of moths than butterflies.

Q. You can often see crowds of swallowtail butterflies on the trail around wet spots or piles of horse dung. What are they doing?
A. They are drinking fluids from urine or dung, possibly to get salt or other nutrients. They also like nectar.

Q. Another butterfly with a taste for horse dung is the Diana fritillary. This species has sexual dimorphism. What's that mean, and what is the advantage of it?
A. Male Diana fritillaries are orange and black. The females are larger than the males, almost as big as a swallowtail, and

Male Diana frittillary

blue and black. Except for the lack of a "tail" on the wing, the female fritillary looks like a pipevine swallowtail, which tastes bad to birds. So if the female lands on the horse dung with a bunch of swallowtails, she is unlikely to get caught by a bird.

Q. Why doesn't the male use that trick, too?
A. Once the male and female have mated, she can store sperm

For more about animals signs, you can get a children's book at a visitor center: Who Pooped in the Park?

and fertilize eggs as long as she can lay them. The males live shorter lives; possibly that's why they do not develop the mimicking coloration.

Fritillary larvae eat violet leaves. The female lays her eggs in fall when violets have no leaves. The larvae hatch and hibernate. They emerge in spring as the violets send out delicious new leaves.

Q. What's a springtail?
A. A small soil invertebrate that can jump many times its own length—there are 210 species in the park, and there may be 100,000 springtails in a square meter of soil and leaf litter.

Q. What newly discovered species of springtail was named for a famous concert pianist and politician?
A. Cosberella lamaralexanderi. which was named after U.S. Senator Lamar Alexander in recognition of his support for the ATBI program.

Q. Can you match each bird with its lifestyle?
Birds:
1) Common Raven
2) Wild Turkey
3) Turkey Vulture
4) Eastern Bluebird
5) Brown-headed Cowbird
6) Barred Owl
7) Goldfinch
Lifestyles:
A) Both male and female call.
B) Mate for life.
C) Males have harems.
D) Nests in fall.
E) Doesn't build a nest—just lays eggs on a rocky ledge.
F) Doesn't build a nest—just lays eggs in other birds' nests.
G) Both the male and female defend the territory.
A. 1-B; 2-C; 3-E; 4-G; 5-F; 6-A; 7-D

Monarch butterflies migrate through the park in September on their way to Mexico.

CADES COVE

The Olivers' cabin

Q. Who were the first white settlers of Cades Cove?
A. John and Lucretia Oliver and their baby daughter, Polly, in 1819.

Q. What was the Cove like then?
A. It was almost completely forested. Cherokees hunted there and may have farmed in small clearings. Cherokees often passed through the Cove on their way from the main town, Kituwah, near the present Deep Creek, to the Overhill Towns in Tennessee.

Lucretia Oliver feared the Cherokees. One night while John was out hunting, she heard people approaching the cabin. She and Polly crouched silently in the farthest corner until the noise stopped. When she finally had the courage to look outside, she found large pieces of dried pumpkin by the door. John had little experience as a hunter, and the gifts from the Cherokees got the family through the winter.

Q. How big is Cades Cove?
A. About 8 miles long (13 km) and 3 mile wide (5 km). The loop road is eleven miles (18 km).

Q. How many creeks flow into Cades Cove?
A. More than 30.

Cades Cove on a stormy day

Q. How many creeks flow out of the Cove?
A. One—Abrams Creek, named for the Cherokee Chief Abram. It flows through the campground, traverses the length of the Cove and then cuts through a beautiful gorge and over one of the most visited waterfalls in the park to meet the Little Tennessee River (Chilhowee Lake).

Q. Who was Cade?
A. Cades Cove may have been named for Kate, the wife of Chief Abram, who lived in Chilhowee, a Cherokee town at the mouth of Abrams Creek.

Q. What is its elevation?
A. About 1750 feet, or 533 meters. It is surrounded by 4000-ft. (1219 m) mountains such as Rich Mountain, Gregory Bald, and Spence Field.

Q. What did the Cherokee call Cades Cove?
A. Tsiyahi, Place of the Otter. Otters were extirpated from the mountains by trappers, but they have been reintroduced, and you can see otters playing and fishing in Abrams Creek and other large creeks of the Smokies.

Q. Why was Cades Cove so appealing to white settlers?

Some of our citizens seem to think that a medicine is no good unless it has whiskey in it. About a gallon to a spoonful of medicine. Cades Cove News, *June 24, 1904*

A. Two reasons: the land is relatively level, and the underlying rock is limestone with a good depth of topsoil. In many mountain settlements, acidic soils limit crops, but limestone soils are more basic. Corn and wheat grew well there, and livestock flourished.

Q. Why did the number of Cades Cove white families increase suddenly in the late 1830s?
A. In 1838 the Cherokees were removed from the area and marched to Oklahoma (the Trail of Tears). Roads could be built through former Cherokee areas, increasing trade and travel to the Cove.

Q. How did the earliest settlers get tools?
A. From 1827 to 1847 a bloomery operated on Forge Creek Road, just past the Cades Cove Visitors Center. It burned charcoal in a simple furnace and made pig iron from local ore which could be shaped into plows and axes, frying pans and barrels. It went out of business when better materials could be bought from outside. The bloomery had 500-lb water-powered hammers, and when they did the job of stamping pig iron into desired shapes, everyone in the Cove could hear them.

Q. Was the Cove isolated from other parts of Tennessee?
A. At first, but as roads improved, people traded farm products for tools, cloth, and other supplies in Knoxville and Maryville. Mail came from Maryville weekly at first and then more often.

Q. What happened in the Cove during the Civil War?
A. Cove settlers, like most people of East Tennessee, sided with
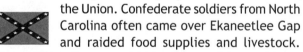 the Union. Confederate soldiers from North Carolina often came over Ekaneetlee Gap and raided food supplies and livestock.
Some Cades Cove men hid in the woods to avoid conscription. A few families went way back to a creek valley and established a colony called New World near the base of Thunderhead Mountain. Other families posted children as home guards at the entrances to the cove—the children would appear to be playing a game, but after any stranger passed they would blow a hunting horn.

"We found all good Union men here. They all have to sleep in the bushes every night...They live in continued terror of being killed [by Confederates]."—A Union soldier helped by Cades Cove farmers

Q. One gravestone in the Primitive Baptist Church cemetery has the epitaph: "Russell Gregory, 1795-1864, Founder of Gregory's Bald about 1830, Murdered by North Carolina Rebels." What's the story?

A. Russell Gregory, like most Cove residents, sided with the Union. His son, Charles, joined Will Thomas' Confederate Legion, which raided Smokies settlements for food and supplies. One night, the legion started to raid the Cove, but the men were driven back by gunfire. Charles Gregory recognized the sound of his father's gun and told the other members of the legion where his father lived. The next night, they sneaked into the Cove, dragged Russell Gregory out of his house, and shot him. Many years later, the family and Cove residents forgave Charles for his betrayal, and you can find his grave behind his father's.

Q. Why did the settlers of Cades Cove and Cataloochee Cove drive their cattle, sheep, mules, and hogs up to the high elevation balds in spring?

A. It does seem like a lot of work. But there were several advantages:
- The balds were cooler in summer.
- Sending the stock away freed up fields for crop growth instead of pasture.
- There were fewer insects and no ticks on the balds.
- The grasses and shrubs of the balds were nutritious.

Cove farmers paid people to stay up on the balds and watch the animals.

Q. When did the settlers get electricity?

A. The first large-scale use of electricity was in Gregory Cave, not far from the Oliver Cabin, which was lit by a generator for meetings, dances, and other community events. During the Cold War, Gregory Cave was designated a fallout shelter and stocked for 1,000 people.

Q. Can we visit the cave?

A. No, all caves in the park are now closed to protect an endangered bat (the Indiana bat) and to prevent the accidental spread of disease to bat colonies. Researchers can enter some caves

---

From Russie Whitehead's account at Burchfield's Store, Cades Cove, 1912: "Tobacco .22 Shirts, socks .90 Tobacco .25 Tobacco .05 Tobacco, Overalls, Sox, Shoes 4.45 Shoe strings .03 Candy..."

with special permits. Volunteers from Bat Conservation International have gated the entrances of most caves.

Q. What was the highest population of settlers in the Cove?
A. In 1928, about 600 people lived in the Cove. But the Park Commission had the right to seize homes within the established park boundary; the Olivers and other families went to court to save their homes; when that failed, they accepted money for their properties. Many of them entrusted the money to regional banks that failed a year or so later in the Great Depression.

Q. How many parcels of land did the Park Commission buy in Cades Cove for the formation of the park?
A. 105. A couple were large timber holdings, but most were small family plots. One was church land that had been deeded to "Almighty God."

In 1962, U.S. Supreme Court **William O. Douglas** visited Cades Cove and wrote a long article, "The People of Cades Cove," in *National Geographic*. John Oliver, great-grandson of the first settler, was his guide, and Harvey Broome, a young law clerk in Knoxville, hiked with Justice Douglas. Douglas interviewed Kermit Caughron and many other Cades Cove settlers or former settlers and described how they made furniture, chimneys, shingles, shoes, raccoon lard, herbal medicines, moonshine liquor, hog hash (head, feet, liver, red pepper, sage, and salt), and hoe cake (cooked on a hoe blade). Douglas also reported on customs of midwifery, language, bear hunting, and cow belling (each cow could be recognized by its owner by sound).

Q. What movies were filmed in Cades Cove?
A. *A Walk in the Spring Rain*, 1970, with Ingrid Bergman and

"Cades Cove is an exquisite creation, whose sights, sounds, and fragrance fill me with wonder."—William O. Douglas, 1962

Anthony Quinn; *The Dollmaker,* with Jane Fonda, in 1984, from a novel by Kentucky writer Harriette Arnow.

Q. Biologists and local folks had good laughs about several incorrect nature scenes in *A Walk in the Spring Rain.* What was the biggest goof?
A. Quinn took Bergman frog hunting—in the dead of winter when frogs are hibernating. But thanks to the magic of Hollywood, frogs were out and about, sitting in the snow.

Q. When were the last cattle removed from Cades Cove?
A. 2000. Some Cades Cove residents had lifelong leases after the park was established, and even after they had all gone, some farmers could lease pastures and hayfields in the Cove. Kermit Caughron maintained several beehives until just a few years ago and sold honey to tourists. Current management of the Cove emphasizes native flora and fauna.

Q. Will the forest take over the cove again?
A. Current park management is to keep the cove open by mowing and burning and replanting native grasses. The deer help, too.

Q. How are the native grasses different from pasture grasses?
A. Cove farmers imported fescues and other grasses that are good for pasturing cows because they form a tough thatch. Native grasses grow in tufts that provide a more varied habitat for wildlife. Imagine that you're a mouse gathering grass seeds when an owl flies over—the native grass tufts would give you a place to dive for cover. (It won't keep the owls from eating—it will just make them work harder.)

> Cades Cove settlers drained boggy areas, reducing habitat for amphibians and other water-loving species. Some of those wetlands at the far end of the Cove have been restored.

Q. How many people visit Cades Cove each year?

A sampling of how Harvey Payne settled his accounts at Burchfield's store: *Credit by eggs .25 Credit by bee's wax .05 Credit by sang [ginseng] .45 Credit by Peas .56 Credit by fur .75*

A. About 2.5 million. In terms of visitation, if Cades Cove were a national park, it would rank 8th in the country.

Q. Doesn't it get crowded?
A. It sure does—sometimes the traffic gets backed up way back on the road to Cades Cove.

Some ways to visit Cades Cove without worrying about traffic:

• Take a ranger-led wagon ride. Look in the *Smokies Guide* for the schedules.
• The Cove is closed to vehicles until 10:00 A.M. on Wednesdays and Saturdays in warm months (check current schedules)—wonderful times for early morning hikes or bike rides. Bikes can be rented at the camp store.
• Take a tour bus from Townsend.
• Go very early on weekdays (except Wednesdays).
• Go in terrible weather (this is not a guarantee that there won't be traffic jams, but sometimes it works, and the Cove is beautiful in any weather).
• Hike the Cove if a winter snow storm closes the road.
• Hike the Cove by moonlight! (The road closes to cars at dusk.)

The park is considering alternatives that may help with the traffic, from options such as a bus system like that of Zion and Bryce national parks to different schedules of road closings. Local hearings have brought out heated discussions about any changes. Stay tuned. Road repairs in 2010 provided some improvements to traffic flow.

Q. What is the first restored building you come to in a drive around Cades Cove?
A. The Oliver Cabin, where John and Lucretia Oliver raised eleven children.

Q. Did all the Cove residents live in log cabins?
A. No. By the time the park was established, most people had frame houses, at first from lumber sawn at the Cable Mill and later from commercial lumber. Early park administrators focused on pre-

---

"...I knew that for me no matter how big the trees grow...back in the hills there will always be an old road that goes to Grandpa's house."—Inez McCaulley Adams, November 9, 1969

Caldwell House in Cattaloochee

serving houses built before 1890. Twelve families held life leases after 1934, and many of their houses have been torn down. In Cataloochee Cove, more of the modern frame houses have been preserved.

Q. What can we do at the Cades Cove Visitor Center?

A. The visitor center, about half way around the 11-mile (18.7 km) loop, has bathrooms, a bookstore, a working mill (Cable Mill), a nature trail, several restored buildings (including a nice cantilevered barn), and events.

Q. Like what?
A. Demonstrations of blacksmithing, mountain music, Old Timers' Day, sorghum molasses making, other Smokies crafts.

Q. What is sorghum?
A. Sorghum is a grain that originated in Africa and was brought to Georgia in 1853. Farmers grew it for cattle food and silage, but sweet sorghum soon became popular as a source of syrup. The plants grow up to 12 feet tall.

> At Cable Mill and Oconaluftee and at various sorghum festivals you can watch a mule or donkey plodding round and round turning a mill as sorghum stalks are fed into a small opening. The mill crushes the stalks and squeezes out the sweet sap, which can be boiled down in large vats. Sorghum tastes like molasses with a slight grassy aftertaste and is very popular on biscuits. In families without a mule, the kids took turns plodding round and round.

Q. Who was Aunt Becky Cable?
A. Aunt Becky Cable (1844-1940) spent her life working in Cades Cove. She never married, but raised her brother's children, could run the mill and the sawmill, plowed her fields, herded her cows up to Gregory Bald, ran a store and boarding house, sheared her

"The secret of America's strength is in people like those in Cades Cove."—William O. Douglas, 1962

sheep, spun the wool to make clothes and coverlets, harvested and put up food for the family.

Q. How did she happen to buy her own coffin some years before her death?
A. One time, in her 80s, she felt poorly and ordered her coffin, paying for it with knitted socks. She recovered and lived to be

Aunt Becky Cable's house

96. She lived in the two-story frame house behind the Cable Mill; you can learn more about her there.

"Spring seeps up the Smokies about 100 feet a day."
—William O. Douglas, 1962

Newfound Gap Road and Clingmans Dome

Q. How many roads cross the park?
A. Only one, the Newfound Gap Road (US 441) between Gatlinburg, Tennessee, and Cherokee, North Carolina.

Q. How long is the Newfound Gap Road?
A. 31 miles (50 km). If you keep on US 441 after Cherokee you could end up in Miami.

Q. Are there any traffic lights in the park?
A. No. There used to be one near Sugarlands Visitor Center, but in the 1970s Superintendent Boyd Evison had it removed because it detracted from the wilderness appearance of the park.

Q. When did the first car cross the mountains?
A. In 1930 Jack Huff and some friends drove a car up to Indian Gap and then took its wheels off and replaced them with rail wheels. They drove the car down the logging railroads to Oconaluftee, startling folks working in the woods and fields.

Q. Why didn't they go through Newfound Gap?
A. Because it hadn't been found yet.

Q. When was the Newfound Gap Road built?
A. 1933.

Q. What climatic changes will we experience driving from Sugarlands Visitor Center to Clingmans Dome?
A. In climate and biological communities you will go from the equivalent of Georgia to Maine or Canada. It will be a lot cooler and more likely to be foggy or rainy. Clingmans Dome is the southern limit of the Canadian vegetation zone. If you take a wildflower walk in March at low elevation, you can find the same flowers blooming in June at high elevation.

Q. What's the difference between a Nature Trail and a Quiet Walkway?

It's not unusual to have snow at Clingmans Dome in April.

A. A Nature Trail has a brochure and numbered stops to identify plants or tell you more about the history and ecology. Most of them are easy loops of a mile or less and may have a bench or two along the way. Try one.

A Quiet Walkway allows you to get away from the road and just wander as far as you'd like—sometimes to a creek or an old house site with a long straight stone wall. Both have signs and pullouts for easy parking.

> Note: For $1 you can get a Newfound Gap Road Auto Tour booklet in any visitor center that gives information on walks, hikes, picnic areas, and much more. You can also buy or borrow an audiotape guide prepared by the Friends of the Smokies—very informative with an extra bonus of traditional music.

Q. What is a bear jam?
A. Well, here's what happens. Someone sees a bear and stops their car. Other cars stop, and people get out to look at the bear. The bear, naturally, runs away, and some drivers run down or up the road to get a better view...and lucky you, back in the stalled traffic, don't see anything. You might as well get out and talk with other folks until a park ranger gets everyone going again.

Q. What should we do if we see a bear while driving?
A. Slow down and drive by. If you want to stop, pull over if possible. Keep windows rolled up.

Q. Can we feed the bear to get a better view? Besides, they look really hungry.
A. No. For one reason, feeding wildlife is a federal offense. For another reason, as rangers say, a fed bear is a dead bear. They estimate that bears that eat human food or trash live half as long as truly wild bears.

Make sure all trash goes in the bear-proof containers that are available at many spots.

There's almost no place to pass on the Newfound Gap Road. So pull over if you're going a lot slower than the speed limit.

Q. Why is there a loop in the road just past the Chimney Tops parking area? Some say they bought too much road and had to tie a knot in it. Others say that the river valley was too steep and narrow in that spot for curves.

A. The first reason came from Wiley Oakley, sometimes called the "Will Rogers of the Smokies," but perhaps even more entertaining. Oakley was born near Scratch Britches Ridge and had a store in Gatlinburg. A great naturalist and hiker, he guided people, including John D. Rockefeller Jr. and Henry Ford, and may have done as much as some of the more prominent park supporters to publicize the value of these mountains.

The loop avoided several dangerous switchbacks. It's about half way up to Newfound Gap, a sort of shoulder of the mountain, with Clingmans Dome as the head, so you can tell the kids that this is the road's bellybutton.

Q. The two tunnels on the Tennessee side were built by the CCC in the 1930s. But cars and RVs got bigger, and tour busses needed both lanes to get through. How did road contractors enlarge the tunnels while preserving the beautiful CCC stonework?

A. They lowered the road.

Q. When?

A. 2000. You can see the lighter new rocks along the road, but they will soon weather and match the CCC rocks.

Q. Just past the first tunnel, there's a parking area on the right that always seems to be crowded. Why?

A. This is the trailhead for Chimney Tops, a very popular hike. It's only two miles, but many people get a surprise when they find out how steep it is. The exposed rock promontories are spectacular but dangerous—hikers often get hurt climbing around. Big holes through the rock gave them the name.

This is also a wonderful place for a short hike—three bridges in the first half mile give great creek views, and it's a good wildflower hike in spring. Sunny boulders under the first bridge provide good seats for dangling your feet in icy creek water.

Q. Before the tunnel, if you look into the forest on the left

---

Wiley Oakley (1885-1954), self-trained naturalist, showed botanists and other scientists where to find the natural resources they wanted to study in the Smokies.

(as you are going up the mountain), you see many smooth-barked trees that rise up straight and seem to be about the same age. After the tunnel, the trees vary, large and small, and seem to be many different kinds. What changed?

A. Those smooth-barked trees are tulip trees mixed with some hemlocks, maples, and black locusts. They are all the same age because they started growing when the farmers of Sugarlands valley left the park in the 1930s. After the first tunnel, much of the forest has not been cut or farmed—you're getting a view of one pride of the Smokies: 100,000 acres of old growth forest.

Chimney Tops

Q. A few miles past Chimneys is another crowded parking lot. Why is it so popular?

A. This is the trailhead for Alum Cave Bluffs Trail—the shortest and favorite climb to Mount Le Conte. This is also one of the best places for a short hike—many creek bridges, wild flowers, Arch Rock, and in 2.5 miles, Alum Cave Bluffs.

Q. Where is Arch Rock?

A. Less than 1.5 miles up Alum Cave Trail. It's a natural arch in Anakeesta rock, formed by freeze-thaw erosion, with steep steps inside and a steel cable to hang on to. Pretty cool, maybe even spooky. And if you go that far, you might as well hike another mile to Inspiration Point, and then just a bit farther to Alum Cave Bluffs.

Q. What's Anakeesta?

A. It's a reddish shale rock that underlies most of the Newfound Gap road at higher elevations. When water seeps between the shale layers, the rock tends to break. Arch Rock, the rock slides you see from Morton Overlook, and the rock exposed by the building of Newfound Gap parking lot are all Anakeesta. The rock contains acid, so road building and other disturbances damage streams. Anakeesta is from a Cherokee word meaning "place of the balsams."

Acid soil supports heath balds—tangles of rhododendron, mountain laurel, sand myrtle, greenbrier, and blueberry. The lowest heath bald can be seen from the road just past Chimney Tops Trailhead.

Q. What caused that rock slide?

A. In 1973, after heavy snow and later rain, a small rock slide widened to show the bare reddish rock face you can see by looking back toward Gatlinburg from several overlooks. A combination of acid rain, death of fir trees, and the weather caused the brittle Anakeesta rock to break and send trees and soil tumbling down. The slide gets wider every year, even as heath plants (laurel, sand myrtle, blueberries) and lichens and mosses try to colonize the surface.

Q. Who is memorialized at the Rockefeller Memorial?

A. Laura Spelman Rockefeller, the mother of John D. Rockefeller Jr. He gave a $5 million matching grant to buy land for the Smokies in her memory.

Q. What interesting wildlife can you see near the Rockefeller Monument in April?

A. Appalachian Trail thru-hikers—the ones that go from Georgia to Maine. Most of them go through the Smokies in late March or April. Some may hitchhike down to Gatlinburg or Cherokee for food and a shower; others cross the road and keep hiking north.

Q. How far have they hiked by the time they get to Newfound Gap?

A. 203 miles (325 km), with 1,958 (3,133 km) miles to go.

Q. If they don't go down to Gatlinburg or Cherokee, where can they get food next?

A. Just after they hike out of the park at Davenport Gap there's a small restaurant called Mountain Mama's. Hikers can shower and resupply there and get what some of them have been dreaming about for many miles: big fat cheeseburgers. From there it's back into the woods until Hot Springs, North Carolina, 30 miles (48 km) farther up the trail.

> The Cherokees called Clingmans Dome "Mulberry Place," and have a legend of a magic lake below the Dome where animals could go when injured.

More than 10,000 people have hiked the entire Appalachian Trail.

Q. What is the most serious form of pollution in the Smokies?
A. Ground level ozone from automobile exhaust, industries, and coal-burning power plants. Ground level ozone damages lung tissue and can bring on asthma attacks. It scars leaves of sensitive plants. Biologists (with the help of kids on school field trips) monitor visible damage to plants and correlate the information with ozone levels.

Q. Where is air pollution most serious?
A. At the higher elevations. The park monitors ozone, sulfates, and particulates constantly and sometimes has to post warnings about unhealthy air days.

Air quality monitors estimate that visibility is about one-quarter today of what it was 50 years ago. On good days, you can see up to 15 miles (24 km), instead of up to 70 miles (112 km). However, Clean Air laws and reduction of auto and power plant emissions are improving the air quality.

Q. When was the Clingmans Dome Tower built?
A. 1960. The curved concrete tower replaced a wooden fire tower.

Q. How much elevation do you gain in the half-mile walk to Clingmans Dome Tower?
A. 330 feet (100 m).

Q. Why does it seem like more than half a mile?
A. Thinner air at high elevation. Even though it's nothing like Colorado, if you come from lower elevation (say Gatlinburg, at about 850 feet (259 m), you will feel the difference. Ground level ozone can also make some people feel breathless. Try one of the benches along the way.

Q. Why are there so many dead trees?
A. The gray skeletons were Fraser firs that died a few decades ago from an infestation of balsam woolly adelgids in combination with air pollution and acid rain.

Signs and profiles on Clingmans Dome Tower identify the mountains you can see...well, sometimes. Fog is common.

As recently as 1970, peaks such as Clingmans Dome, Mount Le Conte, Mount Mitchell, and Mount Guyot had healthy spruce-fir forests similar to those of northern Maine and Canada. The adelgid, an aphid-like Asian insect, spread slowly through the park. You can see some healthy firs from the tower—these trees have been treated.

Spruce needles

Fir needles

Q. How can you tell a fir tree from a spruce tree?
A. They're both evergreens with short (about one inch) needles. Spruce needles are sharp on the end—almost sharp enough to prick your finger. Fir needles are rounded on the end. Also, spruce cones hang down, while fir cones stand up on the twig.

Q. What did mountain folks call spruce and fir?
A. He-balsam and she-balsam.

Q. How high is Clingmans Dome Tower?
A. 45 feet (13 m)

Q. What is the lake you can see from Clingmans Dome Tower?
A. Fontana.

Q. What trails can you see from the Clingmans Dome Tower?
A. The Appalachian and Mountains-to-the-Sea trails. The Appalachian Trail came to this point from Springer Mountain, Georgia (197 miles), and the MTS starts right here at Clingmans Dome.

Q. If you decide to hike back to Newfound Gap from here and have someone pick you up, how far would it be?
A. 7.9 miles (12 km). It's a beautiful, though pretty rocky hike, and not all downhill, because you have to climb Mount Love, Mount Collins, and a couple other peaks that rise above the road.

> Ranger advice for driving down the mountains: Don't ride brakes. Shift down.

A tiny tarantula, the spruce-fir moss spider, lives only in spruce-fir forest.

ACTIVITIES AND ADVENTURES

Q. How many entrances are there to Great Smoky Mountains National Park (GSMNP)?

A. Sixteen—three gateway entrances at Gatlinburg, Cherokee, and Townsend with visitor centers, several with campgrounds (Cosby, Deep Creek, Big Creek, Abrams Creek) and others with great trailheads. In many places you can just walk onto park property.

Q. Where can you buy gas in the park?

A. Nowhere. Make sure you have enough.

Q. How many miles of trail in GSMNP?
A. More than 800 miles.

Q. Are the trails blazed?
A. Only one trail in the Smokies is blazed—the Appalachian Trail, with white 6" x 2" blazes painted on trees. For all other trails, there are signs at trail junctions with mileages to other trails or destinations.

Q. Do we need a map to hike?
A. You should have one, and it only costs $1. In a group of hikers, each member should have a map and know the plan of the hike in case they get separated. Most search and rescue missions end happily with people getting back together after a bit of confusion.

Q. But we can call if we get lost, can't we?
A. *No!* Cell phones don't work in most parts of the Smokies. And backcountry hiking has risks and responsibilities—hikers should know where they're going and have appropriate clothing, food, and water.

Q. Is hiking in the park dangerous?
A. No, but hikers have to take precautions. More than 95% of Smokies visitors do not stray far from their cars. To join the 5%, get a guide book and map and talk to rangers and volunteers who are waiting at every visitor center to give advice.

Q. Do we have to carry water?
A. Yes—or a way to treat water, which many backpackers do. Water in the park may look clear and safe and may still contain bacteria, viruses, or giardia.

Q. What is giardia?
A. It's a protozoan intestinal parasite that can infect humans, wild boars, beavers, and other animals. It causes serious diarrhea and requires treatment. Treat all water. Water provided at Newfound Gap, Clingmans Dome, and other park facilities is safe to drink.

The Backcountry Campsite in Tennessee that is closest to a road: #1, just over 1 mile (1.6 km) from Abrams Creek Ranger Station on Cooper Road Trail.

Q. What else should Smokies hikers be cautious about?
A. Hypothermia—a cooling of the body's core temperature. Hypothermia may occur because of the wrong clothing, getting wet, becoming dehydrated, or not having enough food.

Q. Is hypothermia most common in winter?
A. In the Smokies, hypothermia can happen in any season. It is probably less common in winter because people generally prepare well for winter hikes. Changing weather, elevation changes, and overexertion may surprise hikers. Getting wet is one of the most dangerous things a hiker can do.

One hiker probably saved her life by removing her fleece jacket and wringing it out. She got separated from her group, got lost, and fell in a creek. She survived the night and was rescued the next day. If she had left her clothes wet and kept moving, she probably would have gotten hypothermia.

For families with small children
This is a secret, so don't tell anyone. There are nature trails in every section of the park, and they are just right for kids. And some of them get little use—you can feel solitude even without taking long hikes. Each one has a self-guiding brochure and is less than a mile long.
• Cosby Nature Trail—kids love the log bridges over small creeks that are just their size.
• Spruce-Fir Nature Trail (near Clingmans Dome and a relief from the crowds there) has boards that are fun to walk on (and keep your feet from getting muddy) and wonderful twisty trees.
• Smokemont Nature Trail goes through big fern fields.
• Collins Picnic Area Nature Trail goes along a pretty creek.
• Elkmont Nature Trail shows signs of logging history.
• Cades Cove Nature Trail passes many restored buildings.
• Sugarlands Valley Nature Trail is wheelchair accessible and great for strollers and toddlers.

The Backcountry Campsite in North Carolina closest to a road: #50, on Chasteen Creek Trail, about 1.3 miles (2 km) from Smokemont Campground.

Q. Any other secrets?

A. Ask at the visitor centers—the folks there know where to see the best wildflowers, the closest waterfall, the views.

Q. How long is the Appalachian Trail in the Smokies?

A. About 70 miles (113 km), much of it on the along the Tennessee/North Carolina state line.

Q. Where can we take a short walk on the Appalachian Trail?

A. The Appalachian Trail crosses the Newfound Gap Road right in

front of the Rockefeller Memorial. You can walk north from the Memorial and visit Icewater Springs Shelter in 1.7 miles. This section is wide and very popular. Or you could cross the road and walk south for just a few minutes and get a feel for the remoteness that long distance hikers experience on most of the trail.

Another place is at Clingmans Dome tower. Signs near the tower indicate two short access trails to the Appalachian Trail. Go left (south) for about five minutes to get a great view of an Anakeesta thrust fault that really shows how rocks of the Smokies were pushed northwest by collision with Africa. (Good huckleberries in August, too.)

Q. How long is the whole Appalachian Trail?

A. 2,170 miles (3,600 km) from Springer Mountain, Georgia, to Mount Katahdin, Maine.

The Appalachian Trail:
• goes through 14 states.
• is maintained by volunteers in 32 hiking clubs.
• is a unit of the National Park Service, with headquarters in Harpers Ferry, West Virginia.
• is one of 11 National Scenic Trails.
• has its highest elevation at Clingmans Dome.

It takes about 5 million steps to complete the Appalachian Trail.

Q. If you wanted to complete all the National Scenic Trails in the U.S., how far would you hike?

A. 17,144 miles (27,590 km). That would include, among others, the Ice Age Trail, Pacific Crest Trail, Florida Trail, and the Continental Divide Trail. And that doesn't even include many other long trails—almost every state has one.

Q. What other long trails go through the Smokies?

A. The Mountain-to-the-Sea (MTS) trail goes from Clingmans Dome to Jockeys Ridge State Park on the Outer Banks of North Carolina, 900+ miles. It runs through the Blue Ridge Mountains, and some parts are not complete.

The Benton MacKaye Trail (BMT), named for the man who came up with the idea of the Appalachian Trail in 1921, starts at Springer Mountain, Georgia, and ends at Davenport Gap in the Smokies 300 miles (480 km) later. It crosses the Appalachian Trail at Sassafras Gap near the Twentymile Ranger Station and is an alternate route to reduce crowding on the Appalachian Trail.

Only three—Deep Creek Trail near Bryson City, Gatlinburg Trail near Sugarlands Visitor Center, and Oconaluftee Trail from the Oconaluftee Visitor Center to the town of Cherokee.

Q. Which park roads allow bicycles?

A. All roads open to cars are open to bikes.

Q. How many Smokies trails allow bicycles?

A. Only three—Deep Creek Trail near Bryson City, Gatlinburg Trail near Sugarlands Visitor Center, and Oconaluftee Trail from the Oconaluftee Visitor Center to the town of Cherokee.

Q. What's the leading cause of death for Smokies visitors?

A. Auto accidents. Second cause is drowning, often involving falls from waterfalls. In 2009 there were nine fatalities in the

Cades Cove Campground has a small camp store—the only one in the park. Forget your toothbrush?

park—five from vehicle accidents, two from drowning, and one fall on slippery rocks.

Q. How many campgrounds are there in the Smokies?
A. Ten.

Q. Which one is the highest?
A. Balsam Mountain, at 5310 feet, guaranteed to be cool all summer.

Q. Which campgrounds are open all year?
A. Smokemont and Elkmont.

Q. Where can you camp in the backcountry?
A. You must camp at one of the 88 designated campsites. Camping outside designated campgrounds is not allowed; rangers will issue tickets to campers in unauthorized spots.

Q. Do you need a permit to camp in the backcountry?
A. Yes. There's a permit station at every major park entrance, and you can call the Backcountry Office (865-436-1231) for reservations and information. Rangers do check campsites to see if campers have permits.

Q. What campsite is highest in elevation?
A. The one at Mount Sterling is at 5820 feet (1774 m).

Q. How do you protect your food from bears and raccoons?
A. Each backcountry campsite and shelter has a set of cables that can hang several packs. You are required to use the cables and not keep food or garbage in your tent.

Q. From what song is the following lyric?
Half bear, other half cat
Wild as a mink but sweet as soda pop
I still dream about that.

A. From "Rocky Top," the fight song for all University of Tennessee athletics. Here's the whole verse:

There are 12 shelters (three-sided stone buildings with sleeping bunks) and one campsite on the Appalachian Trail in GSNP.

Wish that I was on good ol' Rocky Top
Down in the Tennessee Hills
Ain't no smoggy smoke on Rocky Top,
Ain't no telephone bills.
Once I had a girl on Rocky Top,
Half bear...

Q. Who sings it this way: 'Once I had me a man on Rocky Top'?
A. Dolly Parton
Here's another good verse:
Once two strangers climbed ol' Rocky Top
Lookin for a moonshine still
Strangers ain't come down from Rocky Top,
Reckon they never will.

Q. "Rocky Top" is a traditional old mountain song, isn't it?
A. No, it was written in 1967 by Felice and Boudleaux Bryant, a husband/wife songwriting team who penned many country & western hits. The song is now the state song of Tennessee and is the unofficial fight song of the University of Tennessee Athletics Department.

Q. So is there really a Rocky Top?
A. Yes, it's between Spence Field and Thunderhead Mountain on the Appalachian Trail. Football quarterback Peyton Manning and Coach Phil Fulmer posed for a University of Tennessee football poster on good ol' Rocky Top.

Q. What is the most remote place in the park in terms of distance from roads?
A. Tricorner Knob, on the Appalachian Trail above Cosby Campground.

Q. What's the Road to Nowhere?
A. From Bryson City, the Road to Nowhere, built in 1959, goes 5.6 miles into the park along Fontana Lake.

Shelter at Tricorner Knob

Q. Where does the Road to Nowhere go?

There are three shelters on other trails: one at Mount Le Conte, one on Kephart Prong Trail, and one at Laurel Gap near Balsam Mountain.

A. Lots of places! First, there's a 1,200-foot-long tunnel used mainly by hikers, and Lakeshore Trail and other trails start here. From Lakeshore Trail you can enter one of the largest road-less areas in the eastern United States, with many backcountry campgrounds and a trail system that connects to Fontana Dam, Clingmans Dome, and Spence Field.

Q. But why is it called that?
A. It's a long story—dating from 1943, when Tennessee Valley Authority (TVA) built Fontana Dam and took land from communities in Swain County, North Carolina, that was not included in the original park plan. The TVA gave the land to the park, but, at the same time, promised the displaced people that a road would be built from Bryson City to Fontana, which would give access to home sites and cemeteries, calling it the North Shore Road.

This road rapidly became famous and controversial. After constructing the first 5.6-mile section into the park, they stopped because of the environmental damage caused by the acidic Anakeesta rock. When this bedrock is exposed and cut, it releases so much acid into streams that fish, salamanders, and other aquatic wildlife cannot live there. Because of the steep ridges, the route of the North Shore Road could not avoid the Anakeesta rock.

At this point the aborted highway became known as "the road to nowhere." It looks like, finally in 2010, the controversy may be settled with a monetary settlement to Swain County and the preservation of a large wilderness area in the park.

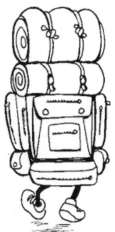

Q. Who was the first to measure Smokies trails?
A. George Masa. He pulled or pushed a bicycle wheel over the trails, counting the revolutions.

Q. Who did the most recent trail measurements?
A. Volunteer Bob Lochbaum, a retired Oak Ridge engineer. He wheeled all trails in the Smokies in both directions at least ten

Lakeshore Trail starts with an abandoned tunnel through Tunnel Ridge. There is a steep Tunnel Bypass Trail for horses spooked by the long, dark tunnel.

times. Then he switched to a large GPS system with a battery pack. Current park maps use his measurements.

Q. What is the steepest trail in the park?
A. According to Bob Lochbaum, Hyatt Ridge, Low Gap, and Mount Sterling trails are the steepest, and Chimney Tops Trail, one of the most used in the park, ranks pretty high, too.

Q. How steep are they?
A. They gain nearly 1,000 feet in elevation in a mile.

Q. What trails start on the Cades Cove Loop Road?
A. Rich Mountain, Cooper Road, Abrams Falls, Wet Bottoms.

Q. What is the Horseshoe?
A. Abrams Creek curves around a ridge to make a horseshoe shape. The trail just goes up and over, but the Horseshoe has a reputation for being: A) one of the best sections for trout fishing, and B) one of the most dangerous off-trail ventures—the creek boulders are slippery and the laurel and rhododendron on the creek banks won't let you out once you're in the Horseshoe.

Hiker's prayer: Oh Lord, You pick 'em up and I'll put 'em down.

Q. How many miles of trail in the park are open to horses?
A. 517, more than half of the trail miles.

Q. How many horse trips are there in the park each year?
A. 80,000, but this includes short trips close to the commercial riding stables.

Q. At 6,593 ft (2,010 m), Mount Le Conte is the third highest peak in the park, However, from its immediate base to its highest peak, Mount Le Conte is the tallest mountain in the Eastern United States, rising 5,301 ft (1,616 m) from its base, near Gatlinburg, Tennessee (1,292 ft/394 m). There are five trails to the top of Mount Le Conte, ranging from 5 miles to 9 miles long, making it one of the most heavily traversed mountains in the park. What is the documented record

---

Trailrider clubs help maintain the trails that horses use.

for the number of times one person has climbed Mount Le Conte?
A. 1,310 times, held by Ed Wright, a retired Oak Ridge engineer.
He did most of the hikes after retirement, about 50 of them after
double knee replacement, and several with his three-year-old
grandson. He died in 2009 at the age of 84.

Other records: Paul Dinwiddie hiked Le Conte 750 times between
the ages of 65 and 80.

Margaret Stevenson hiked it 718 times, along with hiking all
trails of the park. She hiked 50-70 miles per week for nearly
40 years.

Gracie McNicol hiked Mount Le Conte 244 times, including a hike
on her 92nd birthday.

Rufus Morgan hiked Mount Le Conte at least 175 times, the
last on his 92nd birthday.
Three years later, in 1966,
Morgan, along with several
hundred other park lovers,
made a protest hike along
the route of a proposed new
road across the Smokies. The
road has not been built.

Rufus Morgan was an Episco-
pal priest and had an open
air ministry near Franklin,
North Carolina. One time
he performed a wedding
on Myrtle Point (Mount Le

Rufus Morgan Falls

Conte). The wedding parties observed the tradition that the
bride and groom shouldn't see each other until they came
together before the priest, so one party hiked up Trillium Gap
Trail and the other party hiked up Alum Cave Bluffs Trail.

During World War II, most people had a lot more on their
minds than the Appalachian Trail, but Rev. Morgan was too
old to be drafted. He kept about 100 miles of the Appalachian
Trail in North Carolina passable until the younger men came
back from the war.

---

*You can visit Rufus Morgan's church near Standing Indian Campground
in the Nantahala National Forest.*

Q. When did ranger-led naturalist programs start in the park?
A. In 1939, with Park Naturalist Arthur Stupka. He had been a naturalist in Yosemite and Acadia. In the Smokies, he started the Christmas bird count, kept a nature journal, established a herbarium and records of animal specimens, was the first to find several species in the park such as soft-shelled turtles, pine snakes, and a St. Lawrence tiger moth, which he knew from Acadia and recognized as a part of the Canadian Zone of the Smokies. Visitors loved his hikes—88 showed up for one to Ramsay Cascades once.

Q. What is the Parks as Classrooms program?
A. Rangers lead field trips in the park that coordinate with the curricula of North Carolina and Tennessee elementary and secondary schools. Classes visit Mingus Mill, Clingmans Dome, and other areas to study history, geology, biology, or ecology. In 2009 the park started electronic field trips—classrooms all over the country can participate in the on-line trip. Students actually in the park host the program and project microscope views of waterbears, springtails, and other finds.

Q. Every December 3, Mrs. Wanetta Johnson from Johnson City, Tennessee, brings poinsettias to the park rangers at Sugarlands. What is she thanking them for?
A. On Thanksgiving weekend, 1974, her son Eric Johnson and his friend Randy Laws planned to hike from Davenport Gap to Newfound Gap. They reached Tricorner Knob Shelter on their first night out in a snowstorm. The next day they tried to hike out but couldn't get through the snowdrifts and returned to the shelter. The parents contacted the park, which started a search and rescue mission. Snowmobiles and rangers on snowmobiles could not get through, but when the weather cleared, a medical helicopter spotted the boys and dropped supplies. A larger military helicopter came and lifted the boys to safety on December 3, five days after they had been dropped off.

People may panic if they feel lost and try to move faster—a natural response, but it sometimes just gets them more lost.

Q. Many hikers lost for days in winter do not survive. What did these boys do right?
A. • They returned to the shelter.
• They stayed together.
• They had appropriate gear and food for winter conditions.
• They made a sign in the snow for help and placed a red backpack near it to draw attention.
• And, of course, someone (their parents) knew where they were or should be.

Q. In 2009, what did Mrs. Johnson bring to park headquarters besides the flowers?
A. Eric himself, now a 50-year-old lawyer.

Q. How many search and rescue missions are there in an average year?
A. About 100. Most end quickly and happily.

> **1993** was not an average year—a late March blizzard with Arctic temperatures stranded 150 backpackers in the park, several of them on a field trip from Cranbrook School in Michigan, who came south for a nice warm Spring Break. Park roads were closed and the snow was so deep that it covered some shelters. Several backpackers were lifted out by helicopters, and several managed to get out to trailheads on their own, where rangers could drive them to safety. Everyone survived.

Q. How many unsolved disappearances have there been in the park?
A. Three: Dennis Martin, age 6, 1969; Trenny Lynn Gibson, age 16, on a school field trip, 1976; and Thelma Pauline Mellon, age 58, 1981.

Q. How many known and reported plane crashes have there been in the park?
A. 55, the first in 1920, the last (as of this writing) in 2003.

Q. Why so many?

Here's a safety reminder if there's any possibility of getting lost:
S.T.O.P.! (Stop, Think, Observe, Plan)

A. For one thing, the mountains are often socked in with fog or rain. For another thing, early planes did not have sophisticated locators and altimeters, and a slight miscalculation while flying down the Tennessee Valley could be disastrous. Also, some small planes would have enough altitude to clear the mountains but not enough lift to resist downdrafts.

Q. What percent of people involved in park air crashes survived?

A. 44%. OK, that does include the guy whose hot air balloon got tangled in a tree in Greenbrier, and he just climbed down the tree. But most of the accidents involved small planes and pilots who knew how to make emergency landings safer. The few high-speed military aircraft that crashed in the Smokies were fatal.

Q. Can rangers get to a crash site quickly?

A. It is surprisingly difficult to find a crashed plane in the Smokies if there's no locator signal. Planes go in at an angle, so they may be completely concealed, even in winter, by vegetation. Rangers searching from the air look for sheared-off trees. Some

Great Smokies rescue

crashes create a widespread debris field that is hard to see. When the weather is bad, searchers on the ground can't do much.

Plane crashes

Dwight McCarter, a Smokies search and rescue ranger who has written two books about his career, reports that in every case where crash victims were found alive, the rangers were able to get them to safety. In one winter plane crash in 1974, seven people, including three small children, went down in snowy woods near Clingmans Dome. One person was injured, so the pilot, without winter clothes, hiked more than 30 miles for help. He hiked down to Fontana, saw a trail sign

---

For several years, a volunteer ski patrol has worked on the Clingmans Dome Road, which is closed to cars in winter and popular with skiers and sledders.

for Clingmans Dome, hiked back up, then hiked to Newfound Gap and stopped a motorist. Rangers got to the victims in time to rescue everyone.

In one crash of a single-pilot plane in 1998, a group of Boy Scouts backpacking on the Appalachian Trail heard the crash and went into the woods to see what had happened. They found the badly wounded pilot, got him to the trail, and called rescuers.

For one reported crash in January, 1944, the plane and victims have not yet been found. It was a military plane in olive-drab camouflage and carried four people.

The youngest plane crash victim in the Smokies was five-month-old Savannah Dial in 1992. She and her parents had been in Gatlinburg for a Memorial Day vacation. They took off from the Gatlinburg airport in a Cessna 172 and entered thick clouds. The pilot, Savannah's father, became disoriented, and, in spite of help from air traffic controllers in Knoxville, lost control and crashed near the Appalachian Trail at Tricorner Knob.

In 1973 a plane crashed near Mount Le Conte killing all four human occupants, but an Afghan hound survived and was found a week later by students on a hike from an Asheville school.

Q. What are some of the best trails for spring wildflowers?
A. Kanati Fork in April, upper Deep Creek in May, Porter's Creek in March and April, Cucumber Gap in April.

Q. When is Wilderness Wildlife Week?
A. The second week in January. There's a full schedule of hikes and workshops led by experts. It started in 1990 and provides a great way to enjoy safe winter hiking.

Q. When is the Wildflower Pilgrimage?
A. The last week in April. Led by bryologists (mosses), herpetolo-

---

The CCC built trail shelters in the 1930s. The Smoky Mountains Hiking Club started remodeling them in the 1990s, doing one shelter a year with volunteers and support from grants, foundations, and members.

gists (amphibians), arachnologists (spiders), mycologists (fungi), as well as every other sort of expert on biological subjects, this event has taught a lot of visitors about the diversity of the Smokies since its instigation in 1950.

Q. What is the 900-miler club?
A. A club with a website that you can join if you hike all the trails of the park. There are not quite 900 miles of trail in the park, but you will end up hiking between 1500 and 2000 miles to complete those 800+ miles. Here's what happens: you hike several trails and start marking them on a park trail map. Then you'll notice that, if you do just one little section, you'll have done all the Greenbrier trails...Then you see another section of trails you'd like to complete...Soon you're asking your friends to get up at 5:00 A.M. to take you to a distant trailhead...By now you're hooked.... and that's when you join the 900-mile club!

Membership patch

Basic equipment for aspiring 900-milers: an official park trail map and a highlighter.

ABOUT THE AUTHOR

Doris Gove is a biologist, hiker, writer, and editor living in Knoxville, Tennessee, between two great mountain ranges. She has done graduate research on water snakes in the Great Smoky Mountains National Park and has a Ph.D. in snake and lizard behavior. She has taught biology, directed two nature centers, and led hikes and nature programs for Elderhostel, Smoky Mountains Wildflower Pilgrimage, Smoky Mountains Field School, Great Smoky Mountains Institute at Tremont, and many schools.

She has written three hiking guides, all with an emphasis on natural history, and six children's books. The most recent are *My Mother Talks to Trees* and *The Smokies Yukky Book*. She works as a science editor for The University of Tennessee.

Her volunteer work includes volunteering for Appalachian Trail maintenance, service as past president of the Smoky Mountains Hiking Club, and board membership in the Great Smoky Mountains Association and Southern Appalachian Highlands Conservancy.

She is married to Jeff Mellor and has one daughter and one grandson.

Q. Where can you get answers to hundreds of questions about your favorite national parks?
A. In the National Parks Trivia Series!